The Bomber Command Memorial

Published in 2012 by Fighting High Ltd, 23 Hitchin Road, Stotfold, Hitchin, Herts, SG5 4HP
www.fightinghigh.com

British Library Cataloguing-in-Publication data. A CIP record for this title is available from the British Library.

ISBN 978 0 9571163 1 3

Designed and typeset in Monotype Bembo by TruthStudio Ltd, www.truthstudio.co.uk.
Printed and bound by Toppan Printing Co. (SZ) Ltd.

In light of a substantial sponsorship of this book, and for their ongoing support to the
Bomber Command Memorial fundraising campaign, the publishers would like to express their sincere gratitude to
Andrew Hayden and to Sovereign Capital.

The publishers also wish to assert their heartfelt appreciation to The Royal British Legion
for their support of the Bomber Command Memorial campaign and for the sponsorship of this book.

THE BOMBER COMMAND

MEMORIAL

WE WILL REMEMBER THEM

BY ROBIN GIBB • JIM DOOLEY • GORDON RAYNER

STEVE DARLOW AND SEAN FEAST

Contents

Inscriptions on the headstones of RAF
Bomber Command aircrew lost during
the Second World War and buried,
across Europe, in Commonwealth
War Graves Commission Cemeteries.

In Life Loved And Honoured
In Death Remembered

Brookwood Military Cemetery

The Last Full Measure
Of His Devotion

Reichswald Forest War Cemetery

His Memory
Is My Greatest Treasure.
In My Heart
He Lives For Ever

Forenville Military Cemetery

At The Going Down Of The Sun
And In The Morning
We Will Remember Them

Bayeux War Cemetery

He Shall Not Grow Old

Coulonvillers Communal Cemetery

Greater Love
Hath No Man
Than This

Cambridge City Cemetery

May We Be Worthy
Of His Great Sacrifice.
He Died That We Might Live

Andijk Western General Cemetery

Freedom Is The Sure
Possession Of Those Alone
Who Have The Courage
To Defend It

Pericles

This Memorial Is Dedicated
To The 55,573 Airmen From
The United Kingdom British
Commonwealth & Allied
Nations Who Served In RAF
Bomber Command & Lost
Their Lives Over The Course
Of The Second World War

The Fighters Are
Our Salvation But
The Bombers Alone
Provide The Means
Of Victory

Winston Churchill, September 1940

This Memorial Also Commemorates
Those Of All Nations Who Lost Their Lives
In The Bombing of 1939–1945

The Idea

Had it not been for a throwaway comment by Douglas Radcliffe, Secretary of the Bomber Command Association (BCA), on an October day in 2007, the Bomber Command Memorial might well have remained nothing more than a pipe dream in the minds of the surviving veterans.

Standing on the pavement outside the Grosvenor House Hotel on London's Park Lane, Doug was chatting to David Graham, chairman of the Heritage Foundation charity, which had just presented a cheque to the association at one of its regular fundraising lunches. Opposite them was the recently erected £2 million Animals In War memorial, which David was admiring. 'Yes, but where's our memorial?' retorted Doug. 'We never got one.' David was taken aback. 'It just locked into my brain,' he said later. 'I couldn't believe these men had been overlooked.'

So began an unlikely but, as it would turn out, indefatigable alliance between showbusiness and veterans, which would culminate almost five years later in the unveiling of the Bomber Command Memorial in Green Park. The Heritage Foundation, an entertainment industry charity best known for funding blue plaques to remember showbusiness legends, already had an association with Bomber Command going back several years by the time the memorial idea took root. Tony Iveson, a former No. 617 Squadron Lancaster pilot and the then chairman of the BCA, had previously been invited to speak at a lunch to remember the late football com-

mentator Kenneth Wolstenholme (famed for his immortal line 'they think it's all over . . . it is now' in the 1966 World Cup final), who had been a Mosquito pilot during the war and was awarded a DFC and bar. From then on, the Heritage Foundation had made occasional donations to the BCA to help fund its running costs, but, until Doug Radcliffe's chance remark in 2007, no one had thought the link would go beyond that.

The Heritage Foundation's incoming president for 2008 was Robin Gibb, the Bee Gees singer-songwriter who just happened to have a lifelong passion for Second World War history and a particular admiration for the courage of Bomber Command aircrew, partly because of an uncle who had worked in factories building Lancasters during the war. 'I spoke to Robin and told him what a terrible travesty it was that there was no memorial,' said David Graham. 'He said "I quite agree", and I suggested we should do something about it.'

David arranged for Tony Iveson and Douglas Radcliffe to meet Robin at a Heritage Foundation lunch at the Red Lion hotel in Great Kingshill, Bucks., near David's home, which coincidentally happened to be within walking distance of Arthur 'Bomber' Harris's wartime home. 'We talked about Bomber Command, and Robin said he had a project in mind,' said Tony. 'The idea for a memorial came from Robin. It was something we as veterans had talked about in the past, along with the idea of a campaign medal for the bomber offensive, but it needed a catalyst, and that was Robin. He seized on the idea, and something we had felt we couldn't really achieve as a small association suddenly gained momentum.'

Explaining his enthusiasm to get involved, Robin Gibb said: 'It has been a lifelong interest for me, a belief that this country has contributed so much in championing the rights and freedoms of Europe in two world wars. We do a lot of bashing ourselves over the head about our imperial past, but we don't show enough pride in what Britain has done for oppressed people. Growing up in Australia and spending time in America, I saw how loud and proud they were of their men who fought in Bomber Command. These brave men freed Europe, including Germany, from a criminal regime, and it's a simple thing for me to champion because it's really clear-cut that these guys should be honoured. As early as 1940 Churchill said the war would be won in the air and he was right in the end. It was the only force that could bring Hitler to heel. I was born in a free Europe thanks to these guys, and their legacy is that we have lived through the longest peace Europe has known. The memorial will help to set an example to young people about sacrifice, account-ability and pride in a free people. It's also to show young people that democracy is always something you have to champion, and it's never something you should take for granted, it's not a given. I feel like this has been one of the principal quests of my life.'

With Robin agreeing to front the campaign, it was not long before another famous name from the music industry had become inextricably involved. Jim Dooley, whose family pop group The Dooleys scored five Top 20 hit singles in the 1970s, had forged a second career running a not-for-profit organization providing occupational therapy services and equipment to beneficiaries of charities, including forces charities. He had also developed a pas-sion for photography and was one of the country's foremost aviation photographers.

Through these roles Jim had come into contact with Doug Radcliffe, who had come to an arrangement with Jim to sell prints of some of his aviation photographs to raise money for the BCA. 'I grew up in immediate post-war London,' said Jim. 'I played on bombsites and became conscious of a tremendous sense of what is now referred to as the "cup of tea spirit" as people supported each other in times of loss. But there was also a hugely uplifting sense of having come through terrible times together. Ninety people were killed in our street, Westwood Road in Seven Kings, from a dropped landmine that came down on a parachute during the Blitz. But at

Page 8 **Robin Gibb CBE, leading campaigner for the Bomber Command Memorial.** (Mike Partridge via the *Daily Express*) *Left* **Robin Gibb and Jim Dooley.** (Peter Mares) *Below* **Clipping from the *Daily Express*, who were instrumental in raising the profile of the Bomber Command Memorial campaign.** (*Daily Express*) *Right* **The seed of an idea is planted. David Graham of the Heritage Foundation (left), with Doug Radcliffe (centre) and Tony Iveson, in October 2007.** (Doug McKenzie)

school, we were never taught anything about twentieth-century history. We learned of heroic achievements like the success of the Dam Busters from films, comics and, later, TV programmes like *The Valiant Years*.'

Jim also had a personal connection to Bomber Command; his godfather and uncle Stephen Dooley had been a rear gunner in a Halifax with No. 102 Squadron, No. 4 Group Bomber Command, better known as 102 (Ceylon) Squadron, based at RAF Pocklington. 'He survived the war but died very young,' said Jim. 'My father used to speak of his poor circulatory problems, which he said were caused by the extreme cold and stress he was put under as he sat in sub-zero temperatures in his isolated turret.'

Jim first became aware of the significance of the bomber offensive through, of all things, a Russian colonel who was in charge of 'roadies' assigned to the Dooleys when they became the first Western pop band to tour the USSR in 1975. 'He would pour scorn on the western European second front land campaign in the Second World War compared to the great victories at Stalingrad, Moscow and Kursk – except to say that, if it had not been for the contribution of our bomber force, which made it necessary for the Germans to keep a million men back, together with tens of thousands of the dreaded 88mm "ack-ack" guns, plus thousands of fighter aircraft in order to defend their homeland, the Germans would have had the resources available to defeat the Russians early in the war. So that was when I first became aware of Bomber Command's vital contribution to the Allied victory.'

Jim was asked by Doug Radcliffe if he would come along to a meeting with Robin Gibb and the Heritage Foundation to discuss the idea of a memorial, because 'you talk the same pop-speak language as those music people'.

In early 2008 Doug began mustering the people he saw as key to the success of any campaign to build a memorial and summoned them to a meeting in the board room of the RAF Museum in Hendon, at 11.30 a.m. on 4 April. Present at the make-or-break meeting were Marshal of the Royal Air Force Sir Michael Beetham (BCA president), Squadron Leader Tony Iveson (chairman) and Doug Racliffe (secretary) – all of whom were wartime bomber crew – together with Vivienne Hammer (registrar of the BCA) and Tony Edwards (museum trustee). They were joined by Jim Dooley, Robin

Gibb, David Graham, Dave Most (brother of Mickey and manager of Robin Gibb), and Mick Garbutt (Robin's tour manager).

Most of the talking was done by David Graham, who spoke of building a wall with the names of the casualties on, rather like the Vietnam memorial in the USA. It was suggested that Regent's Park would be a good site, as it was close to Lord's cricket ground, where most of Bomber Command's volunteers had been inducted and processed. Someone said it could all be done for about £2 million (there was no architect or design at that stage). Robin spoke passionately about Bomber Command and the part it had played in securing freedom from a 'gangster-style tyranny' that had enslaved most of Europe.

Jim Dooley suggested the Armed Forces Memorial site in Staffordshire would be good place to seek inspiration, because there were many different memorials there, and coincidentally (although no one at the meeting was aware of it) Liam O'Connor, who would later become the architect of the memorial, was at that time finishing the main structure there, a wall that lists the growing number of names of those killed in service since the war.

Jim later recalled: 'I remember walking away from that meeting thinking "Where on earth are we going to get £2m?" Little did I know at the time that from that day we would be chasing a moving target that would eventually top £9m.'

Bomber Command at War

September 1939–October 1940

On 3 September 1939 21-year-old Guy Gibson sat with fellow airmen in his flight commander's office. Tea had been taken, the room was full of smoke, and 'Chiefy' had just informed the young pilots 'all kites ready for testing'. Gibson recalled:

Suddenly the door burst open and Crappy came in. Crappy Kitson looked as though he was about to have a baby. There was something wrong. He did not say much but just went over to the window and turned on the radio. In silence we listened to Chamberlain's solemn words telling the world that a state of war existed between Britain and Germany. So the balloon had gone up. This was war. No one knew quite what to say. Oscar inhaled slowly, then blew the smoke out through his nose. Then he said quietly and rather strongly: 'Well, boys, this is it. You had better all pop out and test your aeroplanes. Be back in half-an-hour's time. There will probably be a job for you to do.'

Over the course of the next five years and eight months 125,000 young Bomber Command airmen would be given a job to do by 'king and country', or perhaps simply 'country' when their homeland became allied to the fight against Nazism. Or perhaps they would take up the cause at a personal level. It could have been the tales of the great aviators from the First World War, their stories of derring-do, that drew them in. Perhaps they simply did not want to be unseamed by a bayonet, having a father's or uncle's experiences to go on. Perhaps they simply did not relish an encounter with water. And to entice them the Royal Air Force recruitment posters offered excitement, purpose, self-esteem, a clean war, and the chance to fight the good cause.

But when the count was finally tallied of those who had become casualties, carrying out what many would describe as simply their job, 60 per cent of them had made a personal physical sacrifice and for 55,573 it was a final sacrifice – including Guy Gibson, who had in the meantime, among other decorations, earned a Victoria Cross. And then there were the emotional sacrifices of those who survived, the deep, suppressed, psychological scars for which statistics were not taken, but may possibly still surface at times of commemoration or remembrance.

Dave Fellowes, who served as a rear gunner, was one of those who had been inspired to take to the air. 'In 1936 Alan Cobham came to a field near us with one of his circuses. I had my first flight then – half a crown for twenty minutes in the air.' Dave joined the Air Training Corps: 'It was right up my street.' Dave, at the age of 16½, would later volunteer for aircrew duties, 'much to my father's horror. He had already seen one war.'

Australian Bill Pearce's dad, a First World War 'Digger', had been clear that he did not want his son to fight the European war. 'He went to France and came home some two and a half years later badly wounded. He virtually walked into a shell burst which blew most of the flesh and muscle from his left leg.' Bill's dad was clear in stating to his son: 'I've been through that once and if I can prevent it, no son of mine will ever have to go through it.' But when it appeared that Bill was actually going to be called up, he persuaded

Above Aircrew recruitment poster.
Right Aircrew of No. 77 Squadron detached to Villeneuve-Vertus, France, pose for a group photograph before boarding their Armstrong Whitworth Whitleys for a leaflet-dropping sortie to Prague and Vienna in January 1940. (Air Historical Branch)

his father that it would be better if he volunteered, to which his father replied: 'You can have a go at joining the Air Force if you like. If anything happens there it will be quick and sudden and you won't have to suffer at length.'

Canadian Jack Watts would cross an ocean with tens of thousands of his fellow countrymen to fight the European war.

There can be no totally common reason why all those young men volunteered for overseas service: such as those from USA who came up to Canada to join the RCAF, those who came from British émigré families in South America and those from first-generation European and British immigrant families in Canada. For those of British origin, it was mainly that they had grown up looking to Britain as the 'home country' and they felt the need to defend her. Universally, though, the images of the destruction being wrought by the powerful Nazi forces on seemingly defenceless cities brought the need to help even more pressing. There was, of course, the personal challenge of fighting a vicious enemy to which young men just naturally responded – gallantly saving the underdog. There was also, of course, that spirit of adventure which appealed to all young men, none of whom wished to miss out on this opportunity.

New Zealander Sidney 'Buzz' Spilman flew a full tour as a pilot with Bomber Command. 'Britain was alone and had to batten down the hatches, making preparations for possible invasion. Germany had had such success everywhere and it was a real threat.' For Buzz and many others in the dominions, it was a case of coming 'to help Britain in a time of need. If you didn't then we were all going down.'

On the first day of the second twentieth-century conflict with Germany, Bomber Command airmen operated against the enemy, searching for German warships. The next day Bomber Command suffered its first casualties, seven aircraft lost, twenty-five airmen killed and two captured on raids against the German fleet. Indeed, in the opening months of the war, raids against German naval vessels were to be the focus, along with the dropping of propaganda leaflets – a period in which the bomber crews acclimatized themselves to the rigours of operations.

Two raids in December 1939 were to cast serious questions

Left **A No. 149 Squadron crew pack their maps into a duffle bag in front of their Vickers Wellington after returning to RAF Mildenhall, Suffolk, following a training flight on 21 December 1939.** (Air Historical Branch)

over the future prosecution of the bomber war. On 14 December, five out of twelve Wellingtons were shot down attacking shipping. Four days later twelve out of twenty-two Wellingtons were lost targeting shipping off Wilhelmshaven. But lessons were yet to be learned, or simply had to be set aside when, in April 1940, German aggression turned towards Denmark and Norway, and, as pilot Wilfred John 'Mike' Lewis recalled: 'It heated up.' Bomber Command attempted to hinder the German assault, and very quickly there was further emphasis of the impracticability of daylight

Below **Squadron Leader C.E. Kay and his crew of New Zealanders serving with No. 75 (New Zealand) Squadron pictured at RAF Feltwell after a raid on Germany in June 1940.** (Air Historical Branch)

bombing in the face of enemy fighter opposition and flak defences. On 12 April, forty-five lives ended as a result of attacking enemy shipping on the Norwegian coast and three more Bomber Command airmen became prisoners; six Handley Page Hampdens and three Wellingtons were lost.

The opening months were proving to be a period when the Royal Air Force's Bomber Command force was having to find its way, both literally and metaphorically; it was having to react both to the realities of operation and to the strategic thinking behind the enemy's moves. During May, and in response to the German Blitzkrieg of Holland, Belgium and France, the Bomber Command Bristol Blenheim and Fairey Battle squadrons, operating in daylight, would suffer terrible casualties attempting to thwart and stifle the German advances. Meanwhile, the Wellington, Hampden and Whitley crews continued operating under the cover of night. As Guy Gibson wrote: 'We home-based Bomber Boys had watched

with a certain amount of trepidation the fate of our poor old Fairey Battles and Blenheims out in France. We had seen them hacked down one by one regardless of individual skill and bravery.' Peter Sarll was a Blenheim pilot on No. 21 Squadron and wrote of the desperate days of May 1940: 'The awful moments I do remember were going back into the village of Watton [in Norfolk] where the young wives were waiting for their husbands who had not returned, and never would.'

At the beginning of June the evacuation of the British Expeditionary Force from Dunkirk was completed, soon to be followed by the final capitulation of France. The western coast of Europe, to the Spanish border, was in German hands, and the Wehrmacht prepared for the crossing of the English Channel. A pre-requisite to such a seaborne crossing was the destruction of the Royal Air Force. The pilots of Fighter Command, however, thwarted the Luftwaffe's attempt to gain control of the skies and their Bomber Command colleagues proved to the German Navy that the RAF had to be defeated. Throughout the period of the Battle of Britain, Bomber Command's operational requirements were wide and varied: attack German industry, particularly oil targets, blast German communications, attempt to burn enemy forests and crops, and attack enemy airfields and aero factories. The aircrews still struggled with the operational difficulties of night-time bombing and dead-reckoning navigation in darkness. Records would later show that these raids had little material effect. There were simply not the means to bomb with accuracy and in large enough numbers. But one campaign during this period did prove to have been significant in deterring German invasion plans: the 'Battle of the Barges', the sustained attack on German shipping assembling in the Channel ports. Indeed, by the end of October 1940 the German Navy had been persuaded of the futility of attempting a Channel crossing without air superiority. Although it did appear that invasion was no longer imminent, attacks on the Channel ports were to continue into 1941.

In the first year of the war Bomber Command had been reacting to German initiative and aggression. Thousands of trained aircrew had been lost fighting a defensive battle. But now, as the nights lengthened, the senior commanders began to take stock of what had been learned, and how this could inform future policy.

'Why the hell can't we go low level into Wilhelmshaven and blast the ships in there?'

Wilhelmshaven 14.12.1939

Newmarket. 3 December 1939. A squadron of Bomber Command's best heavy bomber of the period – the Vickers Wellington – returns to base after a frustrating few days in Lossiemouth. They have been there since 28 November, waiting for Coastal Command aircraft or the Royal Navy's submarines to report on the movement of the German Navy's capital ships. Intelligence suggests that the German pocket battleship *Deutschland* is expected to break out into the Atlantic, but in the event it proves to be a false alarm. A North Sea sweep on 9 December also fails to spot any of the Kriegsmarine's finest.

'Why the hell can't we go low level into Wilhelmshaven and blast the ships in there?' asks one young NCO pilot, 'Tim' Healey.

A pattern of operations is emerging – the 'reconnaissance in force'. One such operation in September ends in disaster, with five

out of the eleven Handley Page Hampdens taking part being shot down. A further attack on two enemy cruisers at the start of December enjoys rather more success, not for any military damage but rather because not a single aircraft is lost. It further strengthens accepted thinking at that time that our bombers are capable of penetrating enemy defences in daylight and emerging unscathed. The Vickers Wellington in particular has enough guns to see off even the most determined fighter attacks. Or so they believe. But the thinking is flawed; fatally so.

Late in the day on 13 December, an RN submarine reports German warships on the move, and a large force of Hampdens and Wellingtons is brought to standby. The Hampdens take off at dawn the following day and return empty-handed. The Wellingtons follow later that same day. The attack is to be made by twelve aircraft.

Above **Wing Commander J.F. Griffiths, the commanding officer of No. 99 Squadron, standing in front of a Vickers Wellington 1A at RAF Newmarket, Cambridgeshire. This photograph was taken on the occasion of the award of the Distinguished Flying Cross to Griffiths for his determined leadership during an attempted attack on a German convoy in the Schillig Roads, north of Wilhelmshaven, on 14 December 1939. Griffiths was also the first Canadian to be given a permanent commission in the RAF since the First World War.**
(Air Historical Branch)

Below Right Wing Commander Richard Kellett, commanding officer of No. 149 Squadron, seated at his desk at RAF Mildenhall, Cambridgeshire. On 18 December 1939, Kellett led a force of twenty-four Vickers Wellingtons drawn from Nos 9, 37 and 149 Squadrons to search for enemy shipping targets in the Schillig Roads off Wilhelmshaven, Germany. The Wellingtons were detected by a German radar station on Wangerooge Island while still on their approach and were subsequently intercepted by fighters. Nine Wellingtons were shot down, three ditched into the sea and a further three were forced to seek alternative landing grounds as they were too badly damaged to return. Kellett was one of those shot down and became a prisoner of war. In January 1940 (when this picture was released) he was awarded the Distinguished Flying Cross for his leadership during the disastrous raid, which, together with that of 14 December, had a major effect on future British bombing policy. (Air Historical Branch)

each armed with three 500lb semi-armour-piercing (SAP) bombs. The advantage of SAP bombs is that they can be devastatingly destructive; the disadvantage is that they cannot be dropped below 2,000 feet, and even at 10,000 feet they might struggle against heavily armoured ships. At that height, accuracy is also an issue. Given the weather forecast – 10/10ths cloud at 1,200 feet, things do not look promising.

The aircraft take off and assemble into four 'Vics' of three aircraft each: numbers two and four sections are astern and stepped down from one and three to provide maximum rearward covering fire, and three and four echeloned to starboard and some 200 yards behind one and two. Control of the formation is to be by wireless telegraphy (w/t), requiring the wireless operators to stay on their sets rather than manning the 'dustbin' turrets that swing down beneath the fuselage of the aircraft. Instead, the dustbins are manned by the front gunners, leaving the front turret vacant. In the lead is the No. 99 Squadron commanding officer, Wing Commander John Griffiths.

Landfall is made just over an hour after take-off, eventually making for the Schillig Roads at a height of little over 200 feet. Flying conditions are difficult, with a thick haze and deteriorating visibility. The formation holds tight, skimming over the top of a group of trawlers and a submarine before turning north-east and sighting two enemy warships almost a mile ahead. The leader makes a wide arc to the left, passing over a number of other vessels that immediately open fire. The cruiser and heavy cruiser also open up with both their main and secondary armament, filling the sky with exploding shells. The formation heads west towards the island of Wangarooge to escape the furore, only to run into a mixed gaggle of Bf109 and Bf110 single-engine and twin-engine fighters – the Luftwaffe's best. For more than twenty minutes a running battle ensues, as the RAF pilots and their gunners fight for their lives, the Germans swooping from above and below in a series of determined attacks. The rear gunner in the wing commander's aircraft fixes a fighter in his sights and blows him out of the sky. He will be awarded the Distinguished Flying Medal for his efforts. But it is the Germans who hold the upper hand.

One Wellington, hit by either flak or fighters, rears upwards and strikes another in formation, both aircraft crashing into the sea.

Another is hit amidships and bursts into flames. A fourth goes down, with the leading edge of the port wing on fire. A fifth is last seen heading for the German coast with its undercarriage down. A sixth manages to limp home, but, with fuel spilling from the Wellington's tanks and the hydraulics out of action, the aircraft dives into the ground short of the landing strip, killing three of the crew. All the other returning aircraft land safely, but all bar one has sustained damage, some of it serious. Moreover, all return without dropping their bombs.

In the fog of war, Wing Commander Griffiths is convinced that his crews have accounted for more of their attackers. By his reckoning, at least four have been shot down: 'It was getting dark and four enemy aircraft burned for some time after hitting the water,' he reports. 'They looked like four enormous beacons.'

Hard lessons should have been learned. But they had not. At least not yet. Four days later, in an almost identical raid, no fewer than twelve Wellingtons are shot down. It is, by any measure, a disaster. German fighters, warned by radar and attacking their enemy on the beam and from above, pursue the Bomber Boys from the target to 80 miles out to sea, and again no bombs are dropped. As the official history remarks pointedly: 'Once more the skill and determination of our airmen left no mark on the German fleet; and this time the cost of failure was even higher than before.'

The Plan

Following the meeting at Hendon in March 2008, the Bomber Command Association agreed to work with the Heritage Foundation and Jim Dooley to take on the task of bringing the idea of a memorial to fruition. Aside from the daunting task of raising funds for a memorial, one of the first hurdles was the task of appointing an architect and agreeing a design.

In August 2008 Jim, Frank Dooley, and Tony Iveson met Lieutenant General Sir Robin Ross, the then chairman of SSAFA Forces Help, who had been involved in dealing with architects for previous memorials. He advised the BCA to approach a number of suitable architects who would be capable of handling such a project. After research by Tony Iveson, the field was narrowed to three candidates: Lord Foster, Donald Insall (who had huge experience of working on historic buildings), and Liam O'Connor, whose work included the Commonwealth Gates on Constitution Hill (just yards from the eventual site of the memorial) and the Armed Forces Memorial in Staffordshire.

All three companies were visited, and in February 2009 the BCA chose and appointed Liam O'Connor, who had won over the committee, not only with his portfolio, but also with his exhaustive knowledge of the processes needed to gain planning permission. 'Liam impressed us the most,' said Jim Dooley, 'because he seemed the most in tune with the cause and he impressed us with his knowledge of the process and the obstacles we would need to overcome in order to secure planning permission.'

Liam O'Connor, David Graham, Sir Michael Beetham, Tony Iveson, and Doug Radcliffe arranged a meeting at the Ministry of Defence with David Forsyth, a civil servant at the MoD, and Squadron Leader Jayne Casebury (a former equerry to the Prince of Wales). Councillor Alan Bradley, a former chairman of one of Westminster Council's planning subcommittees, was also invited, so that the BCA could seek the advice of a senior council representative.

Sir Michael made it clear, in his irresistibly authoritative style, that he did not regard the proposed Regent's Park site as suitable, because he felt the memorial should be more prominent, and closer to the seat of government. But there was a problem (the first of many, as it would turn out).

At a further meeting, this time at City Hall, Westminster, Liam O'Connor, Doug Radcliffe, Tony Iveson, and Tony Edwards met Rosemary MacQueen, the council's head of planning, and council official Mike Gray. At the meeting the BCA was told there was a moratorium policy against further memorials in what was termed the saturation zone. And even though no site had been chosen and no design existed, Mike Gray was already keen to point out that any sculptural element within the memorial would need to be presented to the council's Public Art Advisory Panel for its consideration. Nevertheless, the MoD arranged for the fledgling memorial committee to meet Colin Buttery, deputy chief executive of Royal Parks, and his assistant Mark Wasilewski, to discuss the possibility of building a memorial in one of the Royal Parks. 'I could detect that Colin Buttery wasn't keen on this,' Jim Dooley recalled,

would have the added benefit of being far more prominent, as well as encouraging passers-by to enter the memorial itself. The new site also had the extra appeal of being almost directly opposite the RAF Club, as well as complementing Liam's earlier design at the nearby Commonwealth Gates and removing unsightly railings from the edge of the park.

The feedback from Westminster Council was increasingly positive – Councillor Alan Bradley and others felt it would breathe new life into what had become a neglected corner of Green Park. English Heritage was also supportive of the overall architectural plan, especially its improvements to the streetscape in Piccadilly.

In November 2009 Jim Dooley and Charles Clarke, by now Chairman of the Bomber Command Association, met Liam O'Connor and tree consultant Jeremy Barrell at the proposed site, where Jeremy suggested which trees would need to be removed and how many new ones would need to be planted to satisfy Royal Parks and the council.

Liam O'Connor and Jim Dooley set about approaching potential supporters of the scheme, including the armed forces minister Kevan Jones and the culture minister Margaret Hodge, in order to solicit letters of support that could be presented to Westminster Council's planning committee. Robin Gibb, meanwhile, arranged a letter of support from none other than the Prime Minister, Gordon Brown, after meeting him in Downing Street in June 2009.

On 13 May 2010, the stage was set at Westminster Council's City Hall headquarters on Victoria Street for a showdown that would decide the memorial's fate.

Dozens of Bomber Command veterans, many of them wearing their medals, took their places in a packed planning committee meeting on the seventeenth floor, where the councillors would vote on whether or not to grant permission for building on the Green Park site.

It did not start well. The council's planning officer, John Turner, recommended that the application be refused, partly on the grounds of the council's moratorium on new monuments. He said the proposal 'would cause substantial harm to the special character of the designated heritage asset of the park' because of its 'physical dominance' of the area. Perhaps, he suggested, the committee would agree that 'a more modest proposal', consisting of just a bronze on

'and he talked about the memorial to the Bali bombing, which is sited outside the Parks, behind Whitehall. But we went ahead with a tour of potential sites beside The Mall, and other areas in Green Park, and eventually came to Hyde Park Corner.'

Mr Wasilewski suggested a site on the pavement on the corner of Piccadilly and Constitution Hill, which became the first potential location for the monument. What no one realized at that stage was that the section of pavement in question was actually owned by Transport for London, and was earmarked as a docking site for the 'Boris bikes' that would soon become a feature of London's streets. This only became clear when Liam O'Connor looked into the viability of the site being offered, so it was back to the drawing board for the BCA.

Liam developed a series of options on different locations in the Hyde Park Corner area, including a rotunda-style memorial in the middle of the park. He put this suggestion to the Royal Parks, pointing out that Green Park had plenty of available space. At first, he believed a site in the middle of the park would be the most likely to gain approval from the planners, but Colin Buttery made it clear that Royal Parks would object strongly to such a scheme. Instead, Liam came up with a plan to build the memorial on the edge of Green Park, bordering the pavement of Piccadilly, which

Page 18 A driving force behind the memorial campaign was Bomber Command veteran and former Chairman of the Bomber Command Association Tony Iveson, pictured here at the Green Park site. (Paul Grover) *Left* Bomber Command veterans celebrate outside Westminster Council City Hall on 13 May 2010. (Sam Espensen) *Right* Robin Gibb pops the champagne following the successful meeting at Westminster Council City Hall on 13 May 2010. (Sam Espensen)

They Gave Everything
They Gave Everything
William Clegg

William was killed flying a No. 460 (RAAF) Squadron Vickers Wellington to Mainz on the night of 12/13 August 1942. William's crew of five are buried in Heverlee War Cemetery, Belgium.

a plinth, might be more suitable. He also pointed to letters of objection, most prominently from the Thorney Island Society, a self-appointed conservation group that had been at the forefront of a determined publicity campaign to kill off the memorial for good.

As the veterans shuffled nervously in their seats, it was time for the councillors to have their say. One councillor, Ruth Bush, was swayed by the objections, and regarded the design as 'wholly inappropriate', but she was a lone voice, as others on the committee pointed to two lever-arch files of letters urging support for the site, including a 1,625-signature online petition and letters from the Queen's private secretary and Nick Clegg.

Councillor Louise Hyams said the 'exceptional' design would enhance a 'forlorn and quite ugly part of the park', while Councillor Alastair Moss, chairman of the committee, agreed that a 'bland' corner of Green Park could only benefit from Liam O'Connor's 'very sensitive' plans, which made an 'overwhelming' case for overriding the planning guidelines. He added: 'This is not something to be sheepish about; it is something that needs to make a statement and this is making the correct statement in the correct place.'

After the plans had been approved by a majority vote, Councillor Moss said the memorial would be 'a fitting tribute to the heroes of Bomber Command who made the ultimate sacrifice for our freedom'. He added: 'It is a sign of this country's gratitude to these exceptional people who were brave enough to fight for us and it will stand as an iconic London monument marking how good came to triumph over evil for many generations to come.'

In a statement released by Westminster Council after the meeting, Councillor Moss added: 'This monument has been designed to be in keeping with the nearby classical architecture and its timeless quality should ensure that it soon becomes as synonymous with London as icons such as Marble Arch and Nelson's Column. It is fitting for Green Park, as it will enhance the park, not detract from its appearance, and its size suits its location in Piccadilly. Its elegant and bold design should save the area from being lost amongst the bustle of the city.'

Sir Michael Beetham, sharing champagne with the veterans outside City Hall, beamed: 'At long last we have got people to recognize that we need this memorial. It's what we've been striving for.'

November 1940–April 1942

In **September 1940** British Prime Minister Winston Churchill was adamant: it was necessary to 'develop the power to carry an ever-increasing volume of explosives to Germany, so as to pulverize the entire industry and scientific effort on which the war effort and economic life of the enemy depend'. He was clear that 'in no other way at present visible can we hope to overcome the immense military power of Germany'. In response, the second year of the war, unsurprisingly, found Bomber Command focusing attention mainly on German targets, although there was a four-month hiatus in response to the developments in the North Atlantic.

In January the Command received a directive stating that 'the sole primary aim of your bomber offensive, until further orders, should be the destruction of the German synthetic oil plants'. But the first few months of 1941 are noted for the difficulties the crews experienced operating amid adverse weather conditions. Bomber Command pilot and subsequent holder of the Victoria Cross Leonard Cheshire would write of the nature of operations in early 1941 and the effectiveness of the bombing. 'Overhead a few planes and in them a few bodies. On the ground a few guns, and beside them also a few bodies. The outcome, in essence, is certain. On the ground a few, very few, men and women will lose their lives, a few buildings will be destroyed. In the air, too, a few men will lose their lives, and a few machines be destroyed, possibly.'

But to prosecute the continuing bomber war, new and better performing aircraft were becoming available. On the night of 10/11 February 1941 the four-engine Short Stirlings carried out an oper-

ational debut in the attack on oil facilities at Rotterdam. On 10/11 March 1941 the four-engine Handley Page Halifax entered operational service.

By March 1941 'further orders' were issued in response to the enemy's U-boat and long-range bomber successes in the North Atlantic. The Air Ministry directive to Bomber Command was clear: 'The U-boat at sea must be hunted, the U-boat in the building yard or in dock must be bombed. The Focke-Wulf, and other bombers employed against our shipping, must be attacked in the air and in their nests.' Throughout spring and into the summer of 1941 these 'nests', be they in Germany, or on the Channel coast, were bombarded. Four months after this 'diversion' Bomber Command returned to Germany with the issue of a new directive: 'The weakest points in his armour lie in the morale of the civil population and in his inland transportation system.' The 'main effort of the bomber force' was to be directed at 'dislocating the German transportation system', 'destroying the morale of the civil population as a whole and of the industrial workers in particular'. Targets in Germany's industrial Ruhr would feature prominently in what appeared to be a clear strategic plan. This might have been clear on paper, but in practice and reality it was a different matter.

Canadian Jack Watts had arrived in the United Kingdom in the spring of 1941, and for the rest of the year he steadily increased his operational tally as a Bomber Command navigator.

At that particular time, and one hates to have to admit it, and you didn't know it at the time, the bombing was relatively ineffective. Fifty bombers on a target was a pretty big deal and it would be a very small percentage that were actually on target. You were flying over blacked-out country. You were really pushed in the sense of navigating and finding a target, and dropping the weapons on the target. All you were basically using was dead reckoning with whatever winds you could calculate. On the Whitley, a slow aeroplane, I used astro navigation pretty well on every flight. You had to have your pilot fly straight and level and then whip back down from the astrodome and do your calculations. It was the only way in which you could try and be certain if you were making a good navigational trip. In Europe, when it was blacked out, it was a deadly deal to try and find a target and be sure of what you were doing.

You could try in debriefing to say you felt confident that you were in the target area – the way the searchlights were functioning, the way the flak was concentrated, but was it the right target or wasn't it?

Left Crews of a Bomber Command Bristol Blenheim squadron which was visited by the King and the C-in-C Bomber Command, Air Marshal Sir Richard Pierse, in late 1940, prepare for a night mission following their briefing on the night's targets. (Air Historical Branch)

'Was it the right target or wasn't it?' was the general question posed to a government official in the late summer of 1941. Subsequently, in August 1941, a report was issued that would rock the confidence of the advocates of the bombing offensive. Optimistic reporting of bombing damage was found to be at odds with the evidence accumulated from aircraft bombing photographs. The Butt Report drew its conclusions from an analysis of individual bombing photographs taken during June and July 1941. The statistics were damning. First, one-third of all returning crews were not able to claim an attack on their primary targets. Of the remainder, only one-third came within five miles of the aiming point. Further statistics were equally worrying: on full-moon operations, two in five crews were within five miles of the target, and this worsened to one in fifteen in the absence of moonlight.

A serious rethink was required. Was it worth the effort, the cost, the lives, the aircraft? And, as if to highlight the point, there was the terrible night of 7/8 November 1941, when Bomber Command launched a major attack on numerous targets, despite a dreadful late weather report, the prime focus being Berlin – 392 aircraft were dispatched to all targets that night; 37 failed to return.

Across the winter months of 1941 and 1942, in the light of the Butt Report and operations such as the one of 7/8 November, the future prosecution of the air war was placed under close scrutiny. Operations, for the present, were limited, commanders were replaced, various new reports were commissioned and issued, and senior airmen debated with politicians and other senior military commanders. By February 1942 it was believed some answers had been found. There was the prospect of new and better navigational and bombing equipment, such as Gee, whereby a navigator could obtain a fix with the help of synchronized radio signals transmitted from England. Better performing aircraft would also become available – the four-engine Avro Lancaster would soon make an operational debut. And there was the capacity to expand the front-line strength of the squadrons.

The context for all these developments was that, of all the military forces in the West, Bomber Command was the only force taking the war direct to Germany at this time. On 14 February Bomber Command's future challenge was set out. 'It has been decided that the primary objective of your operations should now be focused on the morale of the enemy civil population and in particular of the industrial workers.' This policy, sanctioned both by the Air Ministry and by government, would undergo a number of adaptations during the rest of the war, but its essence, the targeting of the 'morale of the enemy civil population', would ultimately fuel the post-war ethical debate on the morality of the bomber offensive. Shortly after this 'primary objective' had been stated, a new Commander-in-Chief was appointed, Sir Arthur Harris, who would quickly make it clear that he had no qualms around the validity of escalating the bomber offensive. To keep the bomber battle at the forefront of Allied strategy, Harris would seek to rally his Command, to demonstrate its capabilities, given the right weaponry and manpower, and to force the air war into German skies. He would do so in the most dramatic way in May 1942.

Right NAAFI waitresses serving eager bomber crews, 1941. (Air Historical Branch) *Below* Groundcrew look on as a Handley Page Hampden 1 of No. 408 Squadron RCAF is readied for an engine test in the snow at a dispersal at RAF Balderton, Nottinghamshire, following maintenance on 20 January 1942. (Air Historical Branch)

'A peerless summer day'

La Pallice
24.7.1941

Brest. 21 July 1941. Her refit completed, the German battleship *Scharnhorst* slips anchor and leaves her two companions – *Gneisenau* and *Prinz Eugen* – to steam 200 miles further south to the tiny port of La Pallice on the west coast of France. For some time all three ships have drawn the unwelcome attentions of RAF bombers; now there is the danger that *Scharnhorst* – as yet untouched and undaunted – will escape to the open sea, to wreak havoc on the freighters, oil tankers, and troop ships of the Atlantic convoys. A plan to stop her is needed, and needed fast.

A photoreconnaissance (PR) Spitfire spots her on the morning of 23 July, and Bomber and Coastal Commands attack at dusk, and then again during the night, but with little result. Drastic measures are called for: a daylight attack.

The plan has been in the mind of the commander-in-chief, Sir

Richard Peirse, for some time. The original thought was for a single, decisive raid on Brest, but now this plan has to be adapted to include La Pallice. Brest is attacked by 100 aircraft, a mixed bag of Flying Fortresses, Hampdens, and Wellingtons; the former are intended to draw the German fighters into battle early, to give the 'Wimpeys' a clear run into the target. The Hampdens are even given an escort of Spitfires, while a diversionary raid to Cherbourg by thirty-six twin-engine Blenheims completes the plan – a plan that works in part but not totally. The German controllers are not so easily fooled, and their fighters intercept the Wellingtons in greater numbers than anticipated. A dozen of our bombers are lost in the melee that ensues, although a number of hits on the *Gneisenau* are claimed.

Meanwhile, a force of fifteen of the comparatively new four-engine Handley Page Halifax bombers from two squadrons is on its way to La Pallice. The night before they had taken off from their bases in Yorkshire – with a full bomb load – and stopped over at Stanton Harcourt to refuel. An uncomfortable night for the aircrew sleeping on the hangar floor is considered a small price to pay for the extra bombs they can carry as a result. The defensive firepower of the Halifax is regarded sufficient to withstand fighter attack, even in daylight. A Spitfire escort is in any case out of the question, for they do not have the range for the 600-mile round trip.

At a height of 1,000 feet, and flying in Vic formations, the Halifax force is an impressive sight. The aircraft fly below the German radar screen, undetected. They wait until they are some fifty miles short of the target before climbing rapidly to their maximum ceiling to attack, and enabling their semi-armour-piercing bombs to do their worst.

The weather conditions are excellent, described later by one sergeant observer, 'Monty' Dawson, as 'a peerless summer day... etched in my mind forever'. But then their luck runs out. An enemy destroyer sees them, and sends a signal to shore. Now the element of surprise has gone; the Germans are waiting to greet them with a fierce barrage of anti-aircraft fire and up to two dozen of their best fighters.

Soon the beautiful panorama is full of ugly grey and black puffs of smoke that denote an exploding flak shell from the shore batteries and the *Scharnhorst* herself, each sending hundreds of pieces of burning metal across the sky. The bombers attempt to hold their

Bomber Command Operation Order No. 135

The existing situation at sea makes it essential that the German ships SCHARNHORST and GNEISENAU at BREST should be kept immobilised. Experience has shown that effective night attacks are only possible on comparatively few nights and even then a quite disproportionate expenditure of effort is required to achieve any successful results. In addition the effectiveness of night attacks is likely to be still further reduced by the improved use of smoke screens and searchlights to prevent identification of the ships. It has therefore been decided to stage a large scale attack by day in order to take advantage of the greater precision in bomb aiming which should be possible in daylight.

height and course, but their situation is impossible. In formation they are better able to defend themselves against fighter attack, but can do nothing to avoid the flak. Some break away and are immediately set upon by the fighters, who seem oblivious to the dangers, even of their own flak. Somehow, however, they are still able to complete their bombing run, and at least one stick of bombs is seen to explode in a bright yellow flash close to the ship.

A Halifax goes down in a slow spiral with smoke coming from two engines; only two parachutes are seen. Another is attacked by no fewer than seven Bf109s, all eager to register a 'kill'. Instead the rear gunner accounts for two of their number before he is himself too seriously wounded to continue. With three engines on fire, and a fuselage riddled with flak splinters, the skipper orders his crew to bale out. Five of the seven are wounded. Elsewhere other personal battles for survival end in death; bombers already damaged by flak are easy prey for the Luftwaffe Experten, who have honed their skills in the Battle of Britain the previous year. Three more Halifaxes go down.

At last the surviving bombers turn for home, still hounded by the fighters some distance out to sea until their fuel gauges and ammunition drums oblige them to break off the engagement. It is a long and tortuous journey home, with wounded men on board, instruments shot away, Perspex shattered, and engines overheating or shut down, making their way independently to the nearest airfields on the south-west coast, where they land, exhausted.

By 27 July, all of the men that have made it back to the UK are either safely home at their base in Linton or in hospitals recovering from their wounds. Ted Stocker, a young flight engineer who has helped recover the aircraft, remarks: 'Seeing the crews that made it back, their faces betray the horrors they have witnessed, and the terror they must have felt. Confident, highly trained young men have been sorely tested in battle, and are badly shaken by the experience.'

The men have indeed been tested, and not found wanting. They have also managed to damage the *Scharnhorst* sufficiently to oblige her to return to Brest for repairs. The convoys are at least safe from her guns for a few months to come.

The C-in-C sends a message to all the units involved: 'A magnificent day's work executed with characteristic dash and courage which the world now knows is the tradition of Bomber Command.'

Calton Younger

Royal Australian Air Force

Navigator

Following a **ninety**-three-day voyage, Australian navigator Calton Younger arrived, at the end of August 1941, in Bournemouth, England, with nine other navigator colleagues. 'There were ten of us who had stuck together from training. We became a unit. We were on the same ship. Eight were killed and two became prisoners.'

As a young man Calton Younger was very much aware of what was going on internationally.

I heard Prime Minister Menzies on the radio tell us that Britain had declared war on Germany and therefore Australia was at war with Germany. I was in bed with measles, but I got out of bed and drafted a letter to the Navy. I was that keen. Eventually I got an answer saying that I would be called up in due course but they started up the Empire Air Training Scheme and my father had a friend in the air force who suggested I might like that.

So Cal, who had yet to receive his call-up from the Navy, volunteered to train for aircrew. Like many of his

Australian colleagues, Cal harboured an affinity towards the Empire. 'It was much more important to the dominions than to English people. It was the Empire that I came over to fight for.' Shortly after his arrival at Bournemouth, and having volunteered for Bomber Command, Cal was sent to Lichfield and No. 27 OTU to become part of a crew and gain experience on Wellingtons. It was at Lichfield that the first of Cal's navigator friends became a casualty – his roommate Hal Rogerson.

I was walking back from Lichfield, the airfield was three miles away. I had three-penn'orth worth of chips which I was eating. It was thick fog. I could hear a plane circling. I got home and was lying on my bed reading when a couple of my friends came in and told me that Hal had been killed. They had crashed into a hill in the fog.

In February 1942 Cal joined No. 460 Squadron RAAF, and his first raid to Germany came at the end of March – to Essen. 'I've never seen such a sight in my life.'

We were caught in a cone of searchlights. We saw an aircraft on each side of us go down. They were chucking all sorts of stuff up at us. The second pilot was in the astrodome and he saw a chance to get out. He told the skipper and we did get out of it. They had to put a new wing on the plane.

On 29 May 1942 Cal and his five-man Wellington crew were detailed for a raid on the Gnome & Rhône factory at Gennevilliers, Paris. Cal's pilot, and fellow Australian, Russell Jones, was to fly his bomber into the target at low level, as part of a small force of Wellingtons, 'to light up the target. There wasn't any opposition expected.'

As we approached the target we saw this extraordinary pyramid of searchlights and light flak. It was pretty obvious we were in for a hiding. First of all we were hit amidships and the intercom was put out. I suspect the wireless operator was either

killed or badly injured. I was down at the bombsight, and we were just about on the run-up. I went back to Russ and said we'll bomb on the red and green. I then went back to the bombsight when this stream of light flak appeared to go through the nose – but it must have been in front. It went right along the starboard wing and set it on fire. We were only at 2,000 feet.

I let the front gunner out of his turret, gave him his parachute, opened the trap, and told him to bale out. I grabbed Russ's chute and clipped it on to one side, leaving him to do the other. I picked up my own chute and put that on. Russ said to me, 'Is there any chance?' 'No.' I said. Just then we went into a steep dive. Russ, I could see, was resigned. He was sitting with a little smile on his face. He looked serene.

He said, 'Jump Cal.' I wasn't going to because I didn't think there was a chance. I, too, felt an amazing serenity, but I had nothing to lose so I obeyed orders. Another second would have been too late.

I felt the heat of the fire above me, then the jerk as my parachute opened, just missing a tree. I heard the Wellington crash at the same moment. I went straight into the ground on my chin and knocked myself out for about half an hour – silly as a two-bob watch being dragged by my parachute. When I was coming to I thought, 'Where are all the others. This is a funny sort of heaven.' Then gradually things cleared.

Cal had landed in a commercial vegetable garden. He eventually found his way out and for the next eight days would evade capture before his luck finally ran out. Cal would see out the war as a prisoner. Cal and his rear gunner were the only survivors from Wellington Z1391 UV-R that night.

66 *The building of the memorial and the opening ceremony; the several recent television programmes about Bomber Command, with veterans given their say, and documentaries about the activities at the site of the Great Escape tunnel in Poland; and especially the involvement of Robin Gibb seem to have led to a change in the attitude of many people of the post-war generations towards the bomber campaign. There appears to be acceptance, even vindication of what we did. At the least, there is recognition of the unsurpassed bravery of Bomber Command aircrews.*

People who did not live through the war cannot understand total war, with virtually the whole population engaged in it in one way or another. It was such a completely different way of life. Support for the bomber crews in those suspenseful days was absolute. Many people of recent generations still have reservations, a minority are critical, some even hostile, but most, I believe, accept that what we did must have been necessary. The many young people who approach us to thank us certainly think so. **99**

The Sculptor

Almost as soon as Liam O'Connor had been appointed as the memorial's architect, another vital choice began pressing on the Bomber Command Association – finding the right sculptor to deliver the bronze centrepiece. It was a process that would take a whole year, beginning with a list of thirty of the world's foremost sculptors, which was gradually whittled down by Liam to a shortlist of six.

Liam showed pictures of their work to the Bomber Command Association. Among the pictures shown were the Falklands War memorial in Portsmouth and the Gurkha monument on Horseguards Avenue in London, both by the British sculptor Philip Jackson. BCA secretary Douglas Radcliffe's eyes lit up as he looked through Philip's portfolio. 'That's our man,' he said with decisive finality. 'It was clear that Philip would rise to the occasion,' said Liam. 'When he visited me to talk about the memorial, he understood straight away exactly what was going on and what the strength and grandeur of the design were going to be.'

Philip's impressive body of public sculptures already included such familiar work as the bronze of Bobby Moore outside Wembley Stadium and Sir Matt Busby outside Manchester United's Old Trafford ground. Coincidentally, he had also competed against Liam O'Connor when Philip won the commission for the memorial to the late Queen Elizabeth, the Queen Mother, off The Mall in London, so he was already aware of Liam's abilities. 'When I was first approached by Liam there was a very short brief,' Philip recalled.

'The sculpture was to be non-triumphal, non-jingoistic, just a piece of quiet remembrance. He also added that it had to be the greatest memorial to the Second World War in this country. I added my own phrase – quietly heroic.'

The memorial committee had already set its sights on the idea of a sculpture of a seven-man heavy bomber crew – a daunting task for any sculptor. 'At the time, the proposed unveiling date was November 2011,' said Philip. 'I didn't think it could be done in the time available, so I almost turned it down a couple of times. It kept coming back at me and I looked at my workload and rescheduled and took a deep breath and said I wanted to do it.'

Philip's father, Humphrey Jackson, had been a pilot with No. 102 Squadron, Bomber Command during the war and was later shot down in a Swordfish after transferring to the Fleet Air Arm, ending up in a POW camp in Mali, so Philip had personal reasons for wanting to take on the commission.

But planning permission for the memorial had still not been granted, and there was no guarantee it would be given at all. Philip told the committee the only way he could get the sculpture done in time would be if it gave him the green light straight away. The BCA took a collective deep breath and formally commissioned Philip on 2 March 2010.

Before he had picked up any of his tools, however, Philip spent weeks meticulously researching the uniforms and kit worn by the different members of a typical bomber crew. He spoke to veterans, read books, watched films, and pored over photographs, and quickly discovered that the uniforms were far from uniform in the way the men wore them.

For a start, each member of the crew wore different kit; a rear gunner wore heavy clothing, a buoyancy suit (instead of a Mae West), and sometimes an electrically heated suit, to avoid freezing to death in the sub-zero temperatures inside his isolated turret. A wireless operator, by contrast, sat next to the heater outlet, and wore lightweight clothing as a consequence. (Doug Radcliffe maintains that wireless operators could be identified by the soles of their boots, as one side would be slightly melted where it came into contact with the heater outlet.)

And there were still more variations – many men would continue to wear the kit they were first issued with, often for superstitious reasons, long after it had been replaced by new versions. Individual airmen had their own ways of wearing their kit (often ignoring official advice), meaning that veterans sometimes disagreed over what constituted an accurate portrayal. 'I knew at the beginning that the big elephant trap was that people who had survived would be focusing in on detail all the time and it wouldn't matter to them what the artistic content was if I got a detail wrong,' said Philip. 'I said right from the word go that the only way I could do this thing was if I had every bit of kit and knew who wore what and when they wore it. The RAF Museum in Hendon provided me with everything worn by each member of a bomber crew, so I could become more expert than the veterans in what was worn. The expert at Hendon gave me detailed instructions about who wore what when. The sort of thing you can get wrong is which straps got done up first. I decided to do a crew who were flying in winter, because there was a distinct difference in the amount of clothing worn by the crews in the summer and winter months and I thought the winter clothes looked more dramatic.'

Once he had settled on what he believed to be the best representation of each member of the crew, Philip pinned up black and white photographs of crews, taken next to their aircraft after they had returned safely from operations, in his studio to enable him constantly to check and recheck the tiniest details of a harness, an oxygen mask, or an intercom cable. 'I had quite a lot of letters that were quite angry from people saying "we never wore helmets outside the aircraft" etc. and I would say "I have got 30 photos of men wearing their helmets outside the aircraft." I realized that their memories

were not always that accurate and it would also differ from crew to crew.'

He decided his crew would be one that had just returned from an operation. 'Five of them look to the sky, to the planes that won't return, and two look down to give a feeling of sadness, pathos and grief,' said Philip. 'On their faces you see the fatigue and strain, the joy of having arrived back home again, and the knowledge that they have to go again, and the next day, and the next day. They stand in a tight group, a band of brothers welded by the heat of war.'

Philip produced a maquette, or miniature, in wax, which was well received, and then produced a bigger maquette, which would be his working model. It was taken to Hendon and presented to the committee on 9 June 2010. The meeting was chaired by Sir Michael Beetham and got off to a bad start. 'Even before I unveiled the maquette they knew I had gone for a crew which had just returned from a mission, and they were all set on it being a crew going out on a mission,' said Philip. 'I said my brief called for them being reflective, and you can't be reflective if you're just about to set off. I said it was a group of men relieved to be on the ground but shaken by their experience and they accepted that, they were all 100 per cent behind that.'

Then the hard work really began, as Philip set about sculpting the first figure – the navigator. He began by making a steel skeleton from scaffolding tubes cut and welded together, then shaped the nine-foot tall figure from a ton and a half of modelling clay. The navigator would dictate the style and mood of the remaining figures, so took the longest to complete, at around four months (still much quicker than the norm for Philip, which can be as long as two years).

Veterans were invited to Philip's studio in Midhurst, West Sussex, in July 2010, and some came with preconceived ideas. 'For seventy years those veterans had clung to this particular memory of them flying and it was the most exciting, most dangerous, most earth-shattering experience they had ever had,' said Philip. 'They had guarded those memories for all those years, and some sculptor came along and was given the job of recreating those memories in 3D. It was as if I was meddling with their memories. It was only after they saw it that they became friendly to the idea.'

As he began work on the next figure, Philip fixed nine-foot-high photos of the navigator on his studio wall for reference, to

Page 30 **Sculptor Philip Jackson** (Paul Grover). *Right* **Philip Jackson works on the aircrew maquette.** (Paul Grover)

They Gave Everything
Leslie Schroeder

Leslie's No. 12 Squadron Avro Lancaster failed to return from a raid to Düsseldorf on the night of 25/26 May 1943, with a total loss of life. Les is buried in the Reichswald Forest War Cemetery, Germany.

ensure the style of the remaining figures matched. He drew inspiration for the faces from pictures of aircrew, whose average age was 22 but who 'aged very rapidly' as their slim chances of survival hit them. Some veterans had suggested the faces should be those of Guy Gibson and other famous names, but Philip dismissed the idea: 'It's not a monument to any one person.'

Another problem Philip had to overcome was the fact that crews would disembark carrying large bags and bits of kit that would have cluttered the sculpture, so he decided 'they had dumped their kit on the ground and they are looking for the planes returning'.

Only one tiny detail was added to the original plan for the figures, following a conversation with Harry Irons, a former rear gunner. 'He told me a gunner always carried a handle with a piece of wire and a hook on the end tucked in his boot, and when he was in the aircraft he used it to extend his reach so he could keep cocking and uncocking his guns to stop them freezing up,' said Philip. 'Hendon didn't have one of these things, so I made one and put it in the boot of each gunner.'

During the time he was working on the sculpture, Philip received a letter from a veteran which he found particularly affecting. 'Sometimes when you do these things you wonder who you're doing it for,' reflected Philip. 'But one letter I got summed it up. It was from a veteran who had been on his fourth mission, over Berlin in 1942, when his Halifax was shot down. He and three others baled out and were taken prisoner, while the other crew members died. He never knew exactly what happened to them, so at the age of 80 he went to Berlin and with the help of a local historian and a metal detector, found the crash site. They unearthed some fragments of metal, and some remains of one of the crew. Using DNA testing they determined it was from the flight engineer, and the war graves commission arranged a funeral. It brought closure to him and I realized that the memorial will bring closure to such a lot of veterans.'

After each clay sculpture was completed, the fiendishly complex process of casting the bronze began. Philip made a 'first generation' rubber mould in his studio, which was sent to the Pangolin Foundry near Stroud for a wax cast to be made. Once that had been checked by Philip, the wax cast was used to make a ceramic mould, which was put into an oven to harden, melting the wax, to be replaced by molten bronze.

But the figures were too large to be cast as a single piece – instead the basic figures were cast in five or six sections, with the airmen's straps, harnesses and other details cast separately. The whole figure would then be welded together from as many as sixteen parts, with tiny marks put in the original clay by Philip used as a reference to make sure everything was precisely lined up.

Once Philip had approved the final bronze, it was burnished with wire brushes, then treated with chemicals to give it the desired colour, and waxed to protect it from the elements. After all of the figures had been cast, they were welded onto a bronze base, forming a sculpture that weighed around 8–9 tonnes. 'Bronze lasts longer than any other material,' said Philip. 'There is no reason why it shouldn't be there in a thousand years' time.'

May 1942–February 1943

Sir Arthur Harris was desperate to prove the worth of his Command. In doing so he needed more aircrew and he needed more aircraft. The planned escalation of the bomber offensive filtered down from the operational squadrons through the training programmes. New squadrons needed new crew and existing squadrons had to replace casualties. But casualties were not restricted to just operational duties.

On 26 February 1942, in the mid-afternoon, RAF navigator Gordon Mellor, with his newly formed crew, including Australian pilot Don Jennings, prepared to take off in a No. 27 Operational Training Unit Wellington at RAF Lichfield.

We took off, up to a couple of thousand feet, with Don flying and a second pilot. Over the intercom I heard, 'That engine is dying. We'll feather the prop.' By this time we were more or less on the circuit and over Lichfield. The other engine was on full power but we couldn't maintain height and reported the problem to the control tower. They said, 'make any runway and come in as quickly as possible'. We made sure we got outside Lichfield. We were low. Ahead was the railway line and station and by the time we reached it, I looked out of the side window and the roof of the station was above us. We just cleared the main line and crashed into a field, skidding along the ground before coming to a halt.

We were lucky. When we had realized we were in trouble I went to the front and got the front gunner out of his turret. He was up in the fuselage with us and just as well, because the front turret broke off and rolled 100 yards across the field. The fuselage filled with smoke and the only way out was through the astrodome. The damn thing stuck, but having struggled with it, it swung down. I popped out and slid down the fuselage onto the wing head first. Then a twist round and down. I knew whoever was in the fuselage could come out the same way so I went to the front to see what had happened. Both the pilots got up out of their seats and walked straight out. The whole front of it had gone – quite amazing. Don Jennings was on the ground and said, 'I've hurt my leg.' He had walked out, a few yards, and collapsed – he had a broken ankle.

We went to the back. Everybody had got out except the rear gunner. He was unconscious, in a rather buckled turret. We couldn't seem to do anything with it at all. Fortunately there were some railway workers down on the line and they came up, bringing tools with them, spades, pickaxes, hammers, and asking what they could do. We said could they get him out, the plane is on fire and it could spread – it was a fabric cover. They set about breaking the turret open. The wireless operator and I borrowed a couple of shovels and went to where the engine was on fire. We spent around twenty minutes shovelling earth on to the engine. Petrol was coming out of the broken tanks and the ground was on fire. Eventually there was a shout. They had got him out. By that time an ambulance was there and another vehicle from the airfield. Unfortunately the gunner died. That was a tragedy that night. With the pilot out, injured, and the rear gunner gone, we had to make up a new crew.

It is yet another stark casualty statistic – around 8,000 Bomber Command aircrew were killed in training accidents during the war. The training units had to meet the unrelenting demand for aircrew to fill vacancies in operational squadrons whether caused by

Right **The commanding officer of No. 207 Squadron Wing Commander F.R. Jeffs, wishes his aircrews good luck at RAF Syerston, Nottinghamshire, before they board their aircraft for a night raid to Germany.** (Air Historical Branch)

expansion or by casualties. The units had to make available and maintain the serviceability of aircraft that might have seen better days. And the trainees had to learn their trade in the harsh wartime flying conditions – accepting risks that were deemed necessary in the escalating bomber offensive, risks that cost lives, such as that of the trainee rear gunner on Gordon Mellor's Wellington, Australian Sergeant W. A. Godfrey.

Gordon Mellor's next moves are indicative of this rapid growth and the demand to intensify the bomber war. He would have had no time to recover from the fatal incident at Lichfield. In fact, he was to be involved in yet another training accident. Then shortly after that he found himself part of the largest bombing raid of the war to date. On the night of 30/31 May 1942 Sir Arthur Harris decided to make a statement. He dispatched 1,047 aircraft to Cologne, drawing upon training units to make up the numbers. This was to be Gordon's first operation over enemy territory. The words 'baptism of fire' fit perfectly.

They were building up the aircraft – coming in to stay from other OTUs. A lot of aircraft and additional crews. It was obvious something big was coming up. At the navigator's briefing, in the early afternoon, we got a certain amount of information, to prepare a flight plan, draw up a route on the charts and gather weather details. But it wasn't until the general briefing that we knew the target. The Group Captain was on the stage, with the flight commanders and the squadron leader – the room was packed. They drew the 'curtains' to one side and then everybody knew we were going to Cologne. The Group Captain spoke first. 'Well you can see where you are going now. What you don't know is that we are putting up one thousand planes.'

The raid was very well established by the time we got to Cologne. From fifty or sixty miles away you could see a glow in the sky – bigger and brighter as you approached. There were a number of dummy fires but no mistaking of where we were heading.

Wireless operator John Banfield also flew to Cologne that night in a No. 207 Squadron Lancaster. 'We were due to bomb in the last twenty minutes of the raid, but before we crossed the Dutch coast we could see Cologne on fire. When we got there, there was very little opposition so we bombed quite easily . . . a mass of flame –

really shocking.' In terms of propaganda and within the parameters of a city attack, the raid was a major success, although many of John Banfield's and Gordon Mellor's Command colleagues were on the forty-one aircraft lost that night. Two nights later Bomber Command followed up with a second thousand-bomber raid (actually 956 aircraft were dispatched) and on 25/26 June 1942 Bremen became the target for the third and final thousand-bomber attack.

Of the first two of these raids, Bomber Command pilot Leonard Cheshire wrote:

For the first time in history the emphasis of night bombing had passed out of the hands of the pilots and into the hands of the organizers, and the organizers had proved their worth. In spite of the ridicule of some of their critics, they have proved their worth. They have proved, too, beyond any shadow

Above **Armourers wheel a trolley of 1,000lb Medium Capacity bombs into position for hoisting into Handley Page Halifax II 'LQ-Q' of No. 405 Squadron Royal Canadian Air Force, at RAF Pocklington, Yorkshire. On the right, another armourer is fitting release gear to Small Bomb Containers (SBCs) filled with 30lb incendiary bombs. Photo taken in July 1942.** *Above right* **Sergeant J.B. Mallett, Sergeant H. H. Turkentine and Sergeant R. H. P. Roberts, flight engineer, bomb aimer and rear gunner, respectively, of an Avro Lancaster B Mk I of No. 57 Squadron RAF, eat breakfast in the Sergeants' Mess at RAF Scampton,**

Into the spring of 1943 the Command's strength grew, in terms of manpower, weaponry, and navigational and bomb-aiming technology. The blind bombing device Oboe, whereby bombing or marking release points were signalled from ground stations in England, became available, greatly assisting with the target-marking responsibilities of the Pathfinders. And there was the introduction of H2S, a ground scanning radar, which initially aided the Pathfinders but over a year later would be a standard piece of equipment on every main force aircraft. On New Year's Day 1943 the new No. 6 (Canadian) Group became officially operational, and the numbers of four-engine bombers, with their greater bomb-carrying capacity, swelled the strength positions of the existing groups.

But Germany's ordeal would be delayed. In the opening months of 1943, in response to War Cabinet concerns over the escalation of enemy U-boat successes, the Command attacked German port facilities associated with the U-boats and French coastal bases – to devastate, as their directive stated, 'the whole area in which are located the submarines'.

At the beginning of March 1943, however, it was time for an all-out attack on the centre of German war production.

Lincolnshire, following their return from a night raid. All three were killed with the rest of the crew of Lancaster R5894 'DX-T' when it collided with high tension cables near Scampton upon returning from a raid on Berlin early on 2 March 1943. (Air Historical Branch) *Right* **Prisoners of war at Stalag VIIIB, Lamsdorf, including numerous Polish airmen who had flown with RAF Bomber Command. Third from right is Polish air gunner Joseph Fusniak who was the only survivor of a training crash in January 1942, and similarly the only survivor when his No. 301 Squadron Wellington was shot down in July 1942.** (Joseph Fusniak)

of doubt that given the time the bomber can win the war. Not only have they proved it, they have written the proof on every face that saw Cologne and the Ruhr.

The strategists had successfully changed the emphasis, but it was still the aircrew's task to fight this emphasis in the aerial front line. The thousand-bomber attacks proved a turning point in the war. Another major development materialized in August 1942 with the introduction of the Pathfinders, whereby certain squadrons were taken to form a new force, with the select aircrews detailed to locate and mark targets for the main force attack, utilizing specific pyrotechnics. This proved to be a steep learning curve for the Pathfinder Force, but as the war progressed its capabilities and efficiencies dramatically improved.

'Let him have it – right on the chin.'

Cologne
30/31.5.1942

Below Aerial reconnaissance image taken over Cologne, Germany, after Operation 'Millennium', the first 'thousand-bomber' raid by aircraft of Bomber Command on the night of 30/31 May 1942. (Air Historical Branch)

High Wycombe. 30 May 1942. Air Marshal Arthur Harris, the new commander-in-chief, is sitting at his desk at Bomber Command headquarters, recording a message for the crews taking part in that night's operations: 'The force of which you form a part tonight is at least twice the size and has more than four times the carrying capacity of the largest air force ever before concentrated on one objective,' he said. 'You have an opportunity to strike a blow at the enemy which will resound not only throughout Germany, but throughout the world. Let him have it – right on the chin.'

At shortly before 23.00hrs, the first engines of more than 1,000 RAF bombers at 52 airfields around the UK begin to burst into life. Wellingtons, Whitleys, Hampdens, Stirlings, Halifaxes, Manchesters, and Lancasters thunder down runways and into the air, all heading in the same direction. This is no ordinary night. This is a night where 'Butch' Harris is taking an enormous gamble. If it works, then his plan for an all-out air assault on the Fatherland will at last become a reality; if it fails, then the detractors of Bomber Command – and there are many – will have won the day, and the real value of Bomber Command might never be realized.

The plan – Operation 'Millennium' – is both bold and spectacular and entirely Harris's own. It is not a stunt, but it has public relations value. Up until this point in the war, the largest force dispatched by Bomber Command against a single target has been 228, and the average number available for operations has never been more than 350. Harris, however, has somehow contrived a plan to put 1,000 bombers in the air, on one night, to attack one target.

On the face of it the plan is impossible, but Harris makes it possible by garnering not just operational crews, but also crews who are coming to the end of their training at Operational Training Units or those at the various Conversion Units learning to fly the new four-engine 'heavies'. The response from within his own group means that he is able to raise the required total of aircraft without having to look to other Commands, although he welcomes the four aircraft from Flying Training Command and the contribution of Fighter Command and Army Co-operation Command, who will fly intruder sorties and diversionary raids to keep the German nightfighters occupied.

With the stage set and his force assembled, Harris waits for his opportunity. It finally comes on the night of 30/31 May. Cologne, although not the C-in-C's first choice, is the designated target. Conditions over Germany are not ideal, but this has to be countered against the good weather that his crews will find on their return. Harris plans to put 1,000 bombers, loaded with incendiaries, over the target in three waves, with the assault scheduled to last ninety minutes. In the vanguard are those aircraft equipped with Gee – an exceptional electronic aid that gives a skilled navigator a good chance of accurately finding the target; at the rear are the four-engine 'heavies' with their greater payloads. In the middle come the rump of Main Force, the instructors and instructed, the experienced and the novice, thrown together in the maelstrom of their commander's determination. Never before has such an audacious attack been tried; never before have the stakes been so high.

Steadily the bombers climb into the night, and many report the phenomenon of 'icing' as they fly through the clouds over the North Sea. Ice adds weight to the wings and freezes control surfaces, and in the very worst cases can cause the aircraft to crash. Some are obliged to turn for home, but the majority fly stoically on, aware that they are part of the greatest air armada ever assembled. Over the Dutch coast, the weather improves, and by the time they start their bombing runs on the outskirts of Cologne, the skies have cleared. Visibility is perfect, but so too for the defenders. Searchlights are much in evidence, cockpits suddenly awash with brilliant light as pilots dive and turn to escape their evil attentions. One pilot, Frank Lloyd, later likens being caught in a searchlight to 'lying on top of a bed, in a shop window, totally naked'.

Where there are searchlights, flak is never far behind, and gradually the gunners are finding their range. But their early successes are soon eclipsed by the sheer weight of numbers facing them. Although the first wave meets fierce resistance, this resistance notably declines as the raid progresses. The defences are soon overwhelmed, becoming – as crews would later tell their intelligence officers – weak and confused. And, as the last of the heavy bombers turns for home, rear gunners have a grandstand seat of the huge fires sweeping the target area. 'It was astounding,' remembers Tom Dailey, a wireless op/air gunner. 'The night sky was a swirling fire of red, orange and yellow. Cologne was alight.'

Early the next morning, Mosquitoes overflying Cologne on a 'nuisance' raid are unable to take photographs because of the dense smoke caused by some of the 12,000 individual fires that continue to burn. Over 600 acres of built-up area have been completely destroyed, including a major railway repair shop and 250 factories essential to supporting the enemy war machine. As well as the factories, numerous post offices and telephone exchanges are destroyed or seriously damaged, and 5,500 Germans killed or injured, with a further 60,000 rendered homeless. The supply of all power, gas, and water is seriously affected, as is civilian morale – temporarily at least. As one airman would later remark: 'London at its worst was not a patch on Cologne.'

And what of the cost to Bomber Command? Of the 1,047 aircraft that eventually take part, 40 fail to return, and a further 116 are damaged, a dozen so seriously that they are written off. By a strange quirk, the aircraft from the training groups suffer fewer losses than those from operational squadrons, and within the training groups, the losses to either pupil pilots or seasoned instructors are almost directly comparable.

The attack is more than simply a propaganda victory: significant damage has been caused; losses have been 'acceptable'; and the tactic of 'saturation bombing' created by a 'bomber stream' has been proven to work. The new 4lb incendiary bombs that every aircraft carried have been devastatingly effective. The template for future Bomber Command operations has been set.

George Dunn DFC

Royal Air Force

Pilot

George Dunn flew forty-four operations with Bomber Command, his first tour carried out during one of the most intense periods of the war – April to October 1943. George's interest in the Royal Air Force had been sparked while witnessing some of the action during the Battle of Britain. 'I lived in Whitstable on the North Kent coast and in line with the Thames Estuary, a main route into London for the German bombers.'

When war broke out, George, at the age of 17, volunteered for the Local Defence Volunteers, or Home Guard, as they came to be known. 'By August 1940 the Battle of Britain was in full swing and we were always on the look-out for German pilots who had baled out.' Early in 1941 George decided 'not to wait for my call-up papers' and volunteered for aircrew training as a wireless operator/air gunner. Following an education test and a medical selection board, George was asked if he would consider pilot training. 'I was happy to accept.'

George carried out his pilot training in Canada, was

awarded his wings on 28 July 1942, and by September 1942 was back in the UK, where 'it was now a question of getting used to flying in this country especially at night where our black-out regulations contrasted greatly with the lit-up areas in Canada'. Over the course of the next few months George built up his flying hours on Wellingtons and Halifaxes, and formed his crew. While at a Heavy Conversion Unit, George was sent to No. 10 Squadron 'to receive my baptism of a first raid over Germany'.

It was customary for all pilots to undertake two trips with an experienced crew before taking their own. My two trips were to Essen and Kiel, both heavily defended targets. It was certainly an eye-opener and I thought, 'My God if it is going to be like this we need to be lucky.' I was glad to get them under my belt. My own crew were anxious to know what it was like so I told them to make sure they had plenty of clean underpants!

In May 1943 George and his crew arrived at No. 76 Squadron, and over the course of the next five months he would fly through one of the most concentrated periods of fighting in the hostile skies of Western Europe. Often the target was located in the heavily defended Ruhr, a fact that would be revealed to expectant crews at briefing, where, upon arrival, the target for that night was hidden from the crews behind a curtain. 'When you walked in, the main concern was what the target was going to be. When they drew the curtain back you saw the red ribbon crossing Europe. 'Oh not the Ruhr again." The air battle over Germany was intense, and Bomber Command losses mounted. 'It may sound callous, but you got used to the empty beds next to you. You would go down to flights and it would be, "Oh he didn't make it back last night." You would probably find you were on that night, so you didn't have a lot of time to mull over the loss.'

On 17 August 1943 George's crew found themselves detailed to take part in a particularly important raid. At

the time they were unaware of the exact nature of the target; indeed it was kept a secret from the crew. But this would prove to be one of the most important raids of the war. That night Bomber Command would be sending 596 aircraft to the German secret weapon research station at Peenemünde on the Baltic coast.

When we got into the briefing room and they drew that curtain back, we saw this line go right the way across to, and through, Denmark. Peenemünde? Where's that? What's that all about? We'd never heard of it. We were just told it was a research station and they mentioned important radar. We weren't told it was experimental rockets. At the end of the briefing they said,

'If you don't do the job tonight you'll go back tomorrow night, the night after that and the night after that', which really hit us. You can imagine the reception we would have had on the second night if we had gone back again.

George considers that he was extremely lucky on this sortie. His Group were initially scheduled to go in on the last wave of the attack, but a change of wind meant they were moved to the front of the raid. That night a small force of Mosquitoes had also carried out a diversionary raid on Berlin. 'We went in first and it turned out that we were very lucky. By the time the nightfighters arrived from the south and Berlin, it was the last wave that bore the brunt.' Indeed, Bomber Command lost a total of forty aircraft. But the attack was deemed a success, and the bomber crews did not need to return the following night.

Completing his tour with a raid to Kassel on the night of 3/4 October 1943, a night on which No. 76 Squadron lost four aircraft, George was subsequently awarded the Distinguished Flying Cross. He would return to operations and fly Mosquitoes with No. 608 Squadron, part of the 'Light Night Striking Force', and then with No. 1409 Met Flight.

66 *I think the Bomber Command Memorial is a wonderful idea – when you think of the contribution Bomber Command made to the war effort. I think the chaps who were lost will be looking down now and saying, 'at last we've got some recognition'.* **99**

Jack Watts
DSO, DFC and Bar

Royal Canadian Air Force

Navigator

E**arly in 1941** Canadian airman Jack Watts arrived at RAF Leeming to begin operational service with No. 10 Squadron. Over the course of the next four years Jack would complete a remarkable service as an observer/navigator, flying with four different squadrons, and completing 106 operations, the majority with RAF Bomber Command, but also including a period in North Africa. By the end of the war Jack had been awarded the DSO, DFC and Bar. On Jack's fourth operational trip, on the night of 1/2 October 1941, his crew, flying an Armstrong Whitworth Whitley, went to Stuttgart.

It was a disastrous night with Met so far out, and winds that strengthened and changed in direction. We tried to see the aiming point but, despite prolonged searching, and even using square search procedures, we could not find a city anywhere in our vicinity. We perhaps were overly optimistic for beginners, but we spent too long in the search and with the stronger winds to contend with we just had too little fuel to reach our coast.

With fuel running out, Jack's crew prepared for ditching.

It was just breaking dawn. I lay on the floor up front with Tom, the pilot, when we hit the water. The rest of the crew were amidships at the crash position, with the fuselage door already jettisoned, and poised for a quick evacuation. Even though it was a skilful landing in the dim light and the choppy sea, the impact was deadly. The glass in the nose was smashed and the water poured like a jet under the forward pressure of the aircraft. I was stunned a bit and was unable to get up before I was covered by water. I saw that Tom's safety harness had broken in the impact, that he had hit his head on the instrument panel and was bleeding from a cut on his forehead. I shook Tom and called for him to get up and get out through the top panel, which we had detached before landing. In his stupor, Tom thought that I was already out and struggled to get out through the top panel, looking for me when he stood on the top of the fuselage. Not seeing me there, and dizzy from the impact, he lost his balance and fell into the water between the engine nacelle and the fuselage. By the time I had followed him, he was struggling ineffectually to climb the wing and get back on the top of the fuselage. I had to climb on to the wing and assist him back up. We then walked back along the top of the fuselage towards the escape hatch with the water slowly rising up over our boots as we walked until the aircraft sank beneath us and we joined the rest of the crew in the water.

The wireless operator had fulfilled his responsibility by throwing the dinghy out of the escape hatch as required in the ditching drill, which we had practised assiduously on previous occasions. However, things didn't work out the way they were supposed to. The dinghy reached the end of the lanyard and fell into the water without opening. By good fortune and the grace of God, the wireless operator had a knife in his gear, and he quickly cut the lanyard before the sinking aircraft could pull the dinghy down with it. It was a physical challenge in that cold water to find the toggle of the inflation device and then to turn the dinghy over and to climb on board with the tangled and dangling ropes.

Fortunately, our wireless operator had been able to send out a Mayday and lock his key down before going to the escape hatch. A search had been started, but what we didn't know

was that we had landed in a mined area. Hours later, we were found by a minesweeper at the end of its search, when, in the process of turning back at the edge of the minefield, the captain had caught sight of a coloured flash in his binoculars. We were elated by our rescue, as was the crew of the minesweeper, and, after a clearance by the naval hospital, we were on the train back to base, members of the Goldfish Club. When our report on the dinghy malfunction was reported, they tested all the dinghies in the squadron aircraft and found that the lanyards had been knotted on the wrong side of the eyelet through which it passed and none of them would have functioned properly in an emergency. Correction action was taken and an Air Ministry Order was subsequently published for Air Force-wide action.

On 28 June 2012 Jack Watts attended the dedication and unveiling of the Bomber Command Memorial.

❝ *So much time had passed and so many of the survivors of the Bomber Command campaign had passed away and could not be there to honour their comrades who died in the battle and could not celebrate the commemoration of all those who served so valiantly in Bomber Command. It was a traumatic event, for all of us, as we honoured the thousands who were lost and mourned those friends and squadron crew mates who passed away and now live on only in our and their family's memories. Per Ardua ad Astra was the motto under which we all served and which so appropriately serves them still as the reminder of their gallant service to king and country in a time of national disaster.* ❞

Raising the Funds

Back in April 2008, when the Bomber Command Association first decided to pursue the idea of a memorial, there was no design, no architect and no sculptor, and the project would have gone no further unless the BCA could start raising money.

Just three weeks after that meeting, at which the BCA had set itself the target of finding £2 million, the Heritage Foundation held a lunch for Bomber Command at the Grosvenor House Hotel in Park Lane (where the seed of the memorial idea had first been planted by Douglas Radcliffe in his conversation with the Heritage Foundation's David Graham). Attended by such famous names as Rick Wakeman and Paul Gambaccini, the lunch raised around £17,000 through an auction, mainly of memorabilia donated by Robin Gibb and Jim Dooley, but some of that was absorbed in costs, and it was clear that the net would have to be cast much wider if the target was ever going to be reached.

From the very beginning, the BCA wanted the memorial to be a 'people's memorial', with money donated by members of the public to give it the mandate it deserved. It was time to get the media on board. David Graham mentioned the memorial appeal to Alec Lom, son of the Pink Panther actor Herbert Lom and a journalist at the *Sunday Telegraph*, who wrote an article in March 2008. An anonymous donor came forward with £100,000, which was followed by a further £50,000 from the same person.

The campaign was up and running, but what was needed was a major media offensive to capture the public's imagination, bring in money, and make it a national cause. Unsure of how to go about it, the committee members were pondering the problem when Jim Dooley's next-door neighbour Duncan Butler mentioned to him that the chief reporter of the *Daily Telegraph*, Gordon Rayner, had recently moved to the same village and happened to have an interest in aviation and military history. Jim swiftly arranged to have a chat with Gordon at the local pub. 'This sounds right up our street,' Gordon enthused when Jim explained the plan for the memorial. 'If I can get the editor interested, we could run this as a *Telegraph* campaign.'

Will Lewis, then the editor of the *Daily Telegraph*, unhesitatingly gave the idea his backing, and at a lunch at the RAF Club in Piccadilly Air Chief Marshal Sir Glenn Torpy, the then Chief of the Air Staff, suggested sending Gordon for a flight in the Battle of Britain Memorial Flight's Lancaster to help kick off the *Telegraph's* campaign (a privilege so rare that even Sir Glenn had never flown in Britain's only airworthy Lancaster). Gordon suggested taking the sprightly Tony Iveson on the flight too (Doug Radcliffe had already made it clear that he had spent enough time in bombers for one lifetime, while Sir Michael was too frail to clamber inside the cramped fuselage).

The last time Squadron Leader Iveson had flown a Lancaster on operations, with the legendary No. 617 Squadron in January 1945, his aircraft was so badly shot up by a German fighter over Bergen that three of his seven crew had baled out, certain they were just moments from crashing, only for Tony to keep the stricken bomber in the air long enough to make land in Shetland, earning a DFC for his courage.

After he had come so close to losing his life in a Lancaster, Gordon was unsure how he would react, sixty-three years on, to an invitation to fly in one again. 'I'd love to!' came his excited reply when Gordon rang him at his home in Surrey. His boyish enthusiasm for flying clearly remained undimmed at the age of 89, and so on a misty September morning Gordon and Tony climbed aboard Lancaster PA474 at RAF Coningsby, home of the Battle of Britain Memorial Flight. Half an hour after take-off came a moment of history, as Flight Lieutenant Mike Leckey invited Tony to slide into the co-pilot's seat (the only modern addition to the aircraft) and take the controls; he thus became the oldest man to fly a Lancaster.

When he was back on the ground, tears filled his eyes as he thought anew of the men who never returned home. 'This flight has made me realize for the first time in fifty years just how lucky I am,' he said, 'because, no matter how skilful you were, it was the luck of the draw whether you survived.'

An account of Tony's flight appeared in the *Telegraph* at the end of October to launch the newspaper's 'Forgotten Heroes' fundraising campaign, and produced instant results. Within days of the article appearing, the BCA's usual mailbag of a handful of letters had turned into a deluge of several sacks of mail per day, each containing thousands of donations, almost all accompanied by letters of support and heart-rending stories of lost fathers, brothers, and husbands.

Doug Radcliffe, who had been a wireless operator in Wellingtons during the war, said: 'Two of the members of my first crew are buried in Germany so the letters from people donating money really hit me below the belt. There were so many moving stories from people who had lost everything during the war, and it made us realize just how much the British public was behind us. We had big donations coming in, but we also had pensioners sending in a pound coin, which was all they could spare, and a little girl, whose father had sent a donation, photocopied a gift aid form from the *Daily Telegraph* and sellotaped a 2p piece to it. Almost every donation came with a personal story behind it.'

The BCA had been completely unprepared for the overwhelming volume of letters and donations coming in every day, which were starting to pile up faster than its two regular staff, Doug Radcliffe and registrar Vivienne Hammer, could process them. After Vivienne had spent three hours at the BCA's bank simply paying in cheques, she called for reinforcements, and Barclay's Bank sent staff to Hendon to help process the donations. The cashiers ended up staying for a month, such was the volume of mail coming in.

At the start of October 2008, the appeal total had stood at £189,000; by the end of the year it had passed the £1 million mark, with more than 80,000 letters accompanying donations sent in to Hendon. Meanwhile, Lord Ashcroft, the former Conservative Party Treasurer and a collector of Victoria Crosses, further boosted the campaign by donating £57,000 – or £3,000 for each of the nineteen VCs won by Bomber Command. Other large donations were made anonymously; one donor in Gibraltar sent £100,000 via his lawyer; his identity remains unknown to this day.

As well as raising money, the BCA needed to raise awareness of the campaign and garner support from people in high places. Gordon Brown, the then Prime Minister and an author who had written a book about tales of courage, told the *Daily Telegraph*: 'I have always believed that the 55,000 brave men of Bomber Command who lost their lives in the service of their country deserved the fullest recognition of their courage and sacrifice.' David Cameron, then Leader of the Opposition, said it was time the nation 'finally showed its gratitude' to the men of Bomber Command, whose 'deeds have not been recognized in the way the heroes from the Battle of Britain have been, but their sacrifices were just as great'. Nick Clegg, leader of the Liberal Democrats, paid tribute to the airmen who had 'fought valiantly for their country, following orders by risking their lives in treacherous conditions as part of a strategic offensive' and backed the campaign for 'a fitting memorial'.

The campaign also began to feature on national television news bulletins, with ITN, the BBC, and Sky all running interviews with Robin Gibb and veterans.

With more than half of the original £2 million target now raised, the BCA found ever more imaginative ways of trying to find the remaining cash.

In November 2008 a banquet and auction in Windsor (including a performance by the reunited Dooleys!) raised £13,000, and the following month a range of greetings cards featuring Jim

Page 46 **The Poppy Salute.** (Flipside)
Above **The** *Daily Telegraph* **launches its appeal in support of the Bomber Command Memorial, 28 October 2008.** (*Daily Telegraph*) *Below* **Salute to Bomber Command Banquet programme.** (Simply Photography)

Victory in our crusade to save Bomber Command tribute from the taxman

Dooley's pictures were produced and sold by fine art publisher Sammy Morgan through her gallery in Eton and via mail order, raising tens of thousands of pounds.

On Remembrance Day in 2008, Doug Radcliffe and other Bomber Command veterans heightened awareness of the appeal still further by wearing their original sheepskin Irvine Jackets to the march past the Cenotaph.

Squadron Leader Al Pinner, who was at the time Officer Commanding, Battle of Britain Memorial Flight (BBMF), set himself the target of raising £100,000 for the appeal, and arranged an exhibition of paintings by the aviation and wildlife artist David Shepherd in the hangar at RAF Coningsby, the home of the BBMF. Al Pinner's efforts culminated in a dinner at the Petwood Hotel (which had been No. 617 Squadron's officers' mess in 1944), where David Shepherd, as guest speaker, brought the house down with his mischievous tales of requisitioning everything from Royal Navy ships to RAF bombers to SAS soldiers as subjects for his commissions. In a typical act of generosity, David also donated an original oil painting of one of his favourite subjects, elephants in the Amboseli National Park in Kenya, which raised tens of thousands more through a national raffle. Needless to say, Al Pinner's target was quickly surpassed.

In June 2009 a banquet attended by HRH The Duke of Gloucester at the RAF Museum, held under the nose of Lancaster 'S for Sugar', raised £80,000 (half of which came from the auction of a flight in the BBMF Lancaster), and Robin Gibb and his wife Dwina generously threw a series of annual garden parties at their home in Thame, in Oxfordshire, a former abbey with stunning formal gardens.

But, as the fundraising total crept towards the original £2 million target, it was becoming clear that £2 million, which had in truth been nothing more than a 'guesstimate' by the BCA, was way short of what a memorial would actually cost. By the spring of 2009, when Liam O'Connor was appointed as the architect for the project, the target had almost doubled, to £3.5 million. Months later, the BCA's insistence on an ambitious bronze sculpture of seven aircrew as the focal point of the monument added almost another £1 million.

For the next three years, every time the BCA came close to the latest target, unforeseen costs would increase it yet again. Legal fees alone for the BCA's battle with the planning authorities and for surveys swallowed up £1 million; unexpected problems with the site, such as a gas pipe that had to be rerouted, pushed the cost up still further, and interminable delays caused by the demands of the authorities led to yet more cost increases.

Lurking in the shadows, however, was an unexpected financial headache that would threaten to derail the project for good. A tax rebate for VAT on all memorials with planning permission, which had been brought in by the Labour government, was to expire in January 2011. The BCA had assumed that the Bomber Command Memorial would therefore be exempt from VAT, but to their horror HM Revenue & Customs informed them that, if building work had not started before the deadline, VAT would be payable, which would add almost £1 million to the total bill. Although the government had set up a fund that gave grants to cover the VAT on building materials for memorials, the entire national fund was not enough to cover the VAT on the Bomber Command Memorial.

The BCA, helped by their friends in the media, lobbied ministers to find a way of solving the VAT problem without bending the rules, and, after three years of anxious waiting, David Cameron finally announced in February 2012 that the government would be giving a one-off capital grant of £796,000 to cover the outstanding VAT bill, on top of £204,000 already paid out by the grant fund.

Notwithstanding the VAT fight, there was plenty of good news for the BCA. In June 2010, Lord Ashcroft, determined that the appeal should not falter, generously agreed to provide the final £1 million once the appeal had got within £1 million of the target.

In October of the same year another major media supporter joined the fray when the *Daily Express* began its own campaign to boost the fund. Within months its readers had given £500,000, and the newspaper's owner, Richard Desmond, agreed to match this pound for pound with £500,000 from his own pocket.

Prince William endorsed the *Express*'s campaign by writing an article in which he said: 'Mine is but one among many voices, urging all those who value the freedoms we enjoy today to contribute whatever you feel you can towards the creation of this wonderful monument.'

Everywhere the BCA looked for support, doors seemed to open, thanks to the overwhelming goodwill of the British public towards the appeal. In September 2009 the Ashes-winning England Cricket Team made their own contribution at Lord's, the ground where so many airmen had been inducted into Bomber Command, by allowing the BBMF Lancaster to fly overhead during a one-day match against Australia. Play stopped as the roar of the Lancaster's Merlin engines reverberated around the famous old ground, prompting an emotional round of applause from the crowd and players alike. A picture of the fly-past, signed by both teams, together with a cricket bat, also signed by both sets of players, would later raise £12,000 at a fundraising auction. Sadly, the Lancaster's visit failed to bring any luck to the England side – captain Andrew Strauss was clean bowled with the very next ball!

In December 2009 the committee recruited the services of Flipside, the digital marketing company that had managed to raise £1 million in eight days for the Vulcan to the Sky project. For the next three years, Flipside would run the fundraising website and handle online donations.

Back at BCA headquarters, Tony Iveson had decided to step down as chairman in order to fulfil family commitments that involved spending a long period in Australia, and the man chosen to replace him was Air Commodore Charles Clarke, who had been a bomb aimer when his Lancaster was shot down in 1944. He spent the rest of the war as a prisoner, and helped in the Great Escape while being held in the infamous Stalag Luft III. Charles would, in turn, be replaced as chairman in the summer of 2010 by Air Commodore Malcolm White, who saw the plan through to completion.

For Jim Dooley, two years of spearheading the fundraising drive was taking an increasing toll on his health. In October 2010 he was rushed to hospital suffering from chest pains and diagnosed as having suffered a heart attack. He remained in hospital for a week, undergoing an operation to insert three stents to widen blocked arteries, and for months his ongoing participation hung in the balance.

Although he had been chairman of the BCA for only a matter of weeks, it fell to Malcolm White to take the strain. He felt it was time to take stock of how far the project had come and what the memorial might look like if no more money came in. With a bank balance of around £4 million (compared with a proposed cost of up to £6 million), Malcolm began working out how much of Liam

Previous page, clockwise from top Carol Vorderman addresses gathered guests at the Salute to Bomber Command Banquet. (Simply Photography); **The support of the *Daily Express* bears fruit.** (*Daily Express*); **Bomber Command Aircrew Veterans Group (Sussex) raising funds for the memorial at Squire's Garden Centre** (Cherry Greveson)

Cyril Anderson

All on board Cyril's No. 49 Squadron Avro Lancaster were killed when it was lost on a raid to Mannheim on the night of 23/24 September 1943. Cyril is buried in the Rheinberg War Cemetery, Germany.

O'Connor's design could be kept in view of the shortfall. Out went the proposed roof, wings, lighting, and other details, as well as some of the more expensive materials, to try to make ends meet.

But the memorial had gained a momentum of its own. In November 2010 a most welcome donation came from the Polish Air Force Association, who, in recognition of the contribution made by Polish aircrew serving with Bomber Command, forwarded a cheque for £40,000. For those at the heart of the campaign, a certain element of fate seemed to be taking over. The memorial was destined to be, no matter what stood in its path.

In January 2011, Richard Desmond introduced his friend John Caudwell, the telecoms entrepreneur, to the fundraising committee. John, who had founded and then sold the high street chain Phones 4U, was a qualified pilot and all-round aviation buff who was keen to help make the memorial a reality. Jim Dooley, who was recuperating in South Africa from his heart attack, received a call from a friend of Richard Desmond who told him John Caudwell was keen to make a substantial donation, and made it clear he did not want the memorial to be scaled back because of any restrictions on cost. Asked how much more money was needed to make Liam O'Connor's full design a reality, Jim replied with a figure of £2 million. Several phone calls later, Jim was given an assurance that John would be prepared to meet the full £2 million shortfall. 'If I'm going to put some money into this, I want to make sure it's something we can all be proud of,' he said.

As soon as he returned from South Africa, Jim invited Malcolm White to the RAF Club for lunch, where he said: 'You know all that work you've been doing to scale back the memorial? Well, you can forget about it, because we've got all the funds we need now.' He told Malcolm about John Caudwell's hugely generous offer, which seemed to have brought the curtain down on the fundraising drive. The BCA, however, had reckoned without Westminster Council.

When planning permission had been granted in May 2010, one of the conditions attached to the council's approval had been that a suitable endowment must be in place to cover the cost of maintenance for twenty-five years. The memorial committee set aside £200,000 to this end, but in March 2011 the council dropped the bombshell that it would take charge of maintenance and wanted £2 million up front before final planning consent could be given. 'It was a massive blow,' said Jim Dooley. 'We thought we'd all but crossed the finishing line and suddenly we were looking at having to raise another £2 million, which was as much as we had originally set out to raise for the entire scheme.'

By chance, Jim had been invited to an RAF Benevolent Fund function at the Imperial War Museum the same week, where Sir Rob Wright, controller of the RAFBF, talked about the charity's work in maintaining the RAF's First World War memorial on London's Embankment. The proverbial light bulb lit above Jim's head and he asked Paul Hughesdon, one of the RAFBF's directors, if it would be prepared to consider becoming the guardians of the memorial once it had been built, under terms that would allow sufficient time for a suitable endowment to be raised. In March 2011, the RAFBF's directors agreed to put the plan to their trustees, who approved the idea, which meant the BCA had three years to raise £1.5 million for the RAFBF to maintain the memorial in perpetuity. After much discussion with Westminster Council, its officers agreed the following month to allow the RAFBF to take responsibility for the maintenance.

The drive for further funds continued and on 8 November 2011 Carol Vorderman hosted the Salute to Bomber Command Banquet, a gala dinner at London's Natural History Museum. Over 400 guests enjoyed a Taittinger champagne reception and a banquet prepared by four of London's top chefs. An auction for donated prizes, which included a flight in Canada's airworthy Lancaster bomber, and a Breitling Navitimer Chronograph engraved with the Bomber Command insignia and serial No. 1/1, contributed to a final net profit for the memorial fund of £260,000.

Nevertheless, more unexpected costs continued to increase the total required; the cost of seating, security, ticketing, and policing the unveiling ceremony on 28 June 2012 added a further £500,000.

Three years after the BCA had set out to raise £2 million, the final cost of building, unveiling, and maintaining the memorial had reached £9.5 million, with £8.5 million of that having to be raised by the BCA, once the government's £1 million grant had been taken into account. At the time of publication, the fundraising marathon was still being run, with projects such as this book, to raise the full sum needed for the memorial's maintenance.

March 1943–August 1943

Early in 1943 John Bell arrived at No. 14 Operational Training Unit at RAF Cottesmore to continue his training as a bomb aimer. However, there was one essential matter to be dealt with. He had to crew up, going through a process that became very familiar to most men who served with Bomber Command.

We were all assembled in a hangar, perhaps not quite 100 guys, and we were told to form up in groups of five. We were all milling around wondering what happened next. I was standing with a Canadian navigator looking a bit bemused, and someone came up to us, obviously an air gunner from his brevet, and said, 'Have you got a pilot?' 'No,' we replied. 'Right,' he said, 'I've found a pilot. I've talked to him and he looks all right so come and join us.' We went over, and he said to the pilot, 'I've got two more crew for you; I'll go and find a wireless operator.'

Over the course of the next few months John and his four crew-mates developed as a team, picking up a further two crew members, a flight engineer and a mid-upper gunner, and flying Vickers Wellingtons, Avro Manchesters and Avro Lancasters as they prepared for their entry operational debut as part of the intensifying bomber offensive of 1943, a year in which 2,255 Bomber Command aircraft would be recorded as having failed to return.

Early in February 1943 Sir Arthur Harris had received clear instructions, through what became known as the 'Pointblank' direct-ive. 'Your primary object will be the progressive destruction and dislocation of the German military, industrial and economic system,

and the undermining of the morale of the German people to a point where their capacity for armed resistance is fatally weakened.' Harris would later call the following year's operations his 'main offensive'. Bomber Command would begin by throwing almost everything it had at one main target system, the industrial spread of the Ruhr, which could still be reached under the cover of darkness during the shorter spring and summer nights. Of course the attack was not exclusive – that would have focused the German defences. During this period there was also the extraordinary combination of invention and flying skill, which led to Guy Gibson's No. 617 Squadron breaching the Möhne and Eder dams on the night of 16/17 May.

From March through June and into July of 1943 the offensive was sustained and intense, with records constantly being broken.

On the night of 23/24 May 826 aircraft were sent to Dortmund, a new record for a non-thousand-bomber raid. But this escalation in the scale of attack was matched by an increase in the scale of attrition – from 5/6 March 1943 to 24 July, 1,038 aircraft were lost on operations. Most of the 7,000 airmen on these aircraft would have been killed. But those who did make it through were able to report their experiences.

Ferris Newton, a flight engineer, flew with pilot George Dunn on a No. 76 Squadron Halifax to Cologne on 28 June.

We were hit in the bomb doors by predicted flak and caught by a master searchlight supported by two or three others. There were a few searchlights wandering about, and as we approached they all went out. George seemed

Above left **Operation 'Chastise' – the Dam Busters raid. The Canadians: back row – Sergeant Sutherland, Sergeant O'Brien, Flight Sergeant Brown, Flight Sergeant Weeks, Flight Sergeant Thrasher, Flight Sergeant Deering, Sergeant Radcliffe, Flight Sergeant McLean, Flight Lieutenant McCarthy and Flight Sergeant McDonald. Front row – Sergeant Pigeon, Pilot Officer Taerum, Flying Officer Walker and Sergeant Gowrie.**
(Air Historical Branch)

Above right **WAAF safety equipment assistants working in the parachute section at RAF Snaith, Yorkshire, in June 1943, inspecting MkI lifejackets ('Mae Wests'). Behind them are parachutes hanging up to air after their monthly inspection.** (Air Historical Branch)

to sense something like a trap, and he had just given us all an alert when SNAP – the master searchlights were on us, first time. These master lights were controlled by radar. Then up came three or four other beams and we were coned. George kept his head well down and concentrated on his flying instruments, taking violent evasive action. It's a mistake to look out – you are blinded by the beam and can't see a thing. Having got us coned, up comes the flak. The first burst – dead in front of the nose; the next – just off the port wing. The third was just a hell of a clatter and bang, shook the old kite up a bit, made my hair stand on end, turning my tummy over at the same time and that was that. It seems like hours before you fly out of the beams, but George was taking some very useful evasive action, and we had shaken one or two of the lights off, then the master light went out, and everything was back to normal.

George Dunn's crew would fly their tour through the Battle of the Ruhr, and Ferris recorded time after time: 'the flak was very intense', 'very hot it was', 'they didn't half put up a barrage that night'. 'How on earth we could fly though it and not get hit: it used to beat me.' On 30 July they went to Remscheid:

A cone of searchlights to port with a Halifax in and a cone to the starboard with one in. That left the way clear for us to go through (it's an ill wind) over the target. As we went through, the aircraft on port side was hit by flak and went on fire, the other was going down with smoke and flames coming away from the two port engines and a German fighter following it down. We saw three parachutes open up but no more. It's rather unnerving to see your own kites being shot down. Everyone in A-Apple was very quiet.

At the end of July 1943 and into early August Bomber Command aircrews would be briefed on four separate occasions to attack the city port of Hamburg, responsible for enemy shipping and U-boat production. The bombers were assisted by the introduction of Window, metallic strips dropped from aircraft in great numbers to counter German radar. Within the shroud of false echoes, the bombers could penetrate the German defences in greater numbers and in greater safety, and loss rates fell. The levels of devastation and suffering in Hamburg – a firestorm consuming acres of property and thousands of lives – were unprecedented.

Into August and a series of Bomber Command raids against Italian targets contributed to the Italian surrender in September. On the night of 17/18 August Bomber Command carried out one of the most significant raids of the war, with 596 bombers, controlled by a Master Bomber, flying to the German secret weapon station at Peenemünde on the Baltic coast. Not that the crews knew they were intervening in V-weapon development. Ferris Newton recorded:

It was a beautiful night, with a very bright moon, and the target was not very well defended with flak. But when Jerry found out where the raid was actually taking place, he sent up a host of nightfighters. We bombed from 7,000 feet, almost low level for us chaps, and we were in the first wave in, so we were clear of the target when most of the Jerry fighters appeared. We had been routed as for Berlin, but we turned smartly, dropping low over Peenemünde, so of course Jerry was late in concentrating his forces there. He had held them for the defence of Berlin, just as we had been told he would do. Crews going in the later waves said the sky was full of fighters. Nothing like being first there, catch 'em when they are asleep.

Indeed it was the later waves that scrapped it out with the enemy fighters, and forty aircraft were lost, the majority in the latter stages of the attack. But the raid was a success in terms of damage caused and the resultant delay on the V-2 rocket development programme.

Sir Arthur Harris's attention, however, was now shifting towards the opening of his next large-scale offensive. He was intent, as he put it, on trying to 'burn out the black heart of the enemy'.

This page, top **The crew of a Handley Page Halifax of No. 51 Squadron hand in their parachutes at RAF Snaith, Yorkshire, on their return from a bombing raid on the Ruhr, Germany, in June 1943.** *Left* **Mosquito IV bombers of No. 105 Squadron in May 1943.** *Opposite page* **The crew of Avro Lancaster III, ED831/WS-H, of No. 9 Squadron, captained by Squadron Leader A.M. Hobbs RNZAF, boarding their aircraft at RAF Bardney, Lincolnshire, for a raid on the Zeppelin works at Friedrichshafen, Germany, during the night of 20/21 June 1943. This special raid introduced novel tactics devised by 5 Group, among which was the 'shuttle' technique. After bombing the target, the Lancasters flew to Blida in North Africa, where they were refuelled and rearmed, returning to the UK two nights later and attacking La Spezia, Italy, en route. Six days later, Hobbs and his crew were shot down and killed in ED831 while returning from a raid on Gelsenkirchen, Germany.** (Air Historical Branch)

'Just checking that my family are all back.'

Peenemünde
17/18.8.1943

15 May 1942. Flight Lieutenant Donald Steventon is flying high over the western shores of the Baltic on a photo reconnaissance (PR) sortie. Far below he notices an airfield and switches on the camera for a short run. When developed, his photographs show heavy constructional works and a number of unusual circular embankments. Seven months later, and reports begin to reach London that the Germans are embarking on a series of secret weapons trials. They confirm a rumour known within the inner circles of British Intelligence and first detailed in the 'Oslo Report' in 1939 that these weapons may include rockets, but the information is 'filed' pending future reference.

It is another three months before a section of photographic interpreters at Medmenham is told to look out for evidence of secret weapons, and the film from the Baltic coast is recalled to mind. A report is prepared for the Chiefs of Staff, and the Prime Minister himself takes a special interest in the new threat to the nation's security. Further photographs are ordered, although the results are baffling. They do not know then that two entirely separate 'Vengeance' (V) weapons are being developed. Then at last a PRU Mosquito returns with some especially high-quality shots that reveal the unmistakable outline of a rocket, and suddenly the significance of those circular embankments is realized. It sets in motion a train of events that will lead to one of the most spectacular and successful of all Bomber Command raids of the Second World War – the attack on the rocket research establishment at Peenemünde.

The raid is planned in extraordinary detail. It must succeed at all costs. Crews are told that, if they miss the target, they will have to go back. They are told that it could help shorten the war, but then they have heard that one before. The target is so secret that they are told simply that the Germans are developing a new radar device, and it must be destroyed. After flying missions to Berlin or the Ruhr, experienced crews are not much impressed. As one Canadian pilot, Jack Stephens, was to remark: 'Peenemünde? No one had the slightest idea where it was or what it was. But we were to find out.'

Group Captain John Searby, an experienced bomber pilot and officer commanding No. 83 Squadron, is given the task of leading what will be a comparatively low-level and no doubt dangerous attack. More than this, he is appointed 'Master Bomber' – a new

Left Annotated aerial reconnaissance photograph taken of Test Stand VII at the Army Research Centre at Peenemünde in northern Germany. Two anti-aircraft positions can be seen on top of the pre-launch facility at the upper right (A); two empty rocket trailers are bottom right (B) and at bottom centre (C) is a V2 rocket on its trailer. (Air Historical Branch)

position that requires him to 'control' the raid with two deputies from start to finish, to ensure that, as far as possible, every bomb hits the target and none of their effort is wasted.

Three specific targets are identified: a housing estate (where the scientists and their families live); the production works; and the experimental works. Bomber Command's Nos 3 and 4 Groups are detailed to attack the residential buildings; No. 1 Group is to bomb the production facilities; and Nos 5 and 6 Groups (the latter an all-Canadian group operating Lancasters for the first time) are allocated the experimental works. Pathfinders are to open the attack, and 'shift' the marking of the aiming points as the raid progresses.

The attacking force comprises almost 600 aircraft, with a further 8 aircraft carrying out a 'spoof' raid on Berlin to fox the German defences. And it works. For the first stage of the attack, all goes well, although the early markers fall short and an unfortunate number of forced labourers are killed. Searby quickly rights the wrong, and the main targets are soon swamped. A smokescreen appears too late to serve any purpose. Some 1,500 tons of high explosive lay waste vast areas of the site, and two out of the first three waves are virtually unmolested – even though the attack takes place in brilliant moonlight.

Then at last the German nightfighters do arrive, angered by their earlier diversion, and set about the third wave of the bomber stream. As well as their frustrations, they have a new, terrifying weapon in their armoury, Schräge Musik: twin, upward-firing canons that enable them to attack from behind and below – in the bomber's blind spot – and rake an aircraft from back to front without being seen. They are to wreak havoc in the months that follow until their secret is at last revealed and new tactics deployed to negate their advantage.

A total of forty aircraft are shot down – an 'acceptable' loss rate given the importance of the target. The Canadians might have cause to think differently, for they suffer worst: twelve of their number are shot down – a proportion expressed as 19.7 per cent of the total 6 Group contingent. As one navigator, Bob Charman, recalls: 'All over the sky planes were going down in flaming infernos.' His aircraft is numbered among those missing, and only he and one other survive.

Running battles are fought as the Bomber Boys head towards

home. Crews are already tired, but it is now that their vigilance is most in demand. At last they arrive at their respective bases, are debriefed, eat, and make for their beds. At one station, a WAAF orderly comes quietly round and pulls down the sheet from each sleeping face. She is asked what she is doing: 'Just checking that my family are all back,' she says.

The ends do indeed justify the means. As well as the structural damage, a number of important scientists and engineers are killed. The V-2 experimental programme is put back by at least two months and maybe as many as six, and the raid is later said to have reduced the scale of the eventual rocket attack. Who knows how many more innocent civilians might have been killed had it not been for the accuracy and expertise of the bomber crews that night.

Right **Test Stand VII following the attack by Bomber Command.** (Air Historical Branch)

John Bell MBE, DFC

Royal Air Force

Bomb Aimer

At the end of June 1943 John Bell arrived at No. 619 Squadron and prepared to carry out bomb-aiming duties.

We had been training for nearly two years and were anxious to put it all into practice – even though it was going to be pretty dangerous, you didn't really think about that. The whole crew had this attitude that we were going to survive; it's not going to happen to us.

In 1936 John had moved with his family to Epsom in Surrey and for the early part of the war John worked in London. In 1940, as the war in Europe began to escalate, John developed an 'interest in the Battle of Britain and what was going on around us. I got caught in one air raid with bombs dropping the other side of a street. I knew I was going to be called up – with the raids on London we were directly involved.' On occasions John would meet some of his older friends who were on leave. 'They had joined up and they told us how great it was flying with the RAF, flying Whitleys.'

During the 1930s I had seen the film of the Great War, with the troops coming out of the trenches and marching across all this mud. It was not something I really wanted to do. I was going to fly.

In June 1941 John cycled into Worcester Park, 'and I volunteered my services'. He wanted to be a pilot, but when measured John was told he was too tall: 'You'll never get out of the aeroplane.' So he was told he had to be a navigator. John travelled to South Africa to carry out his training. Then in early 1943 he returned to the UK and was sent to No. 14 Operational Training Unit at RAF Cottesmore, now detailed to be a bomb aimer. Training at OTU continued on Vickers Wellingtons,

followed by a posting to a conversion unit to fly Avro Manchesters briefly and then Avro Lancasters and finally on to No. 619 Squadron. For just over a year John would then be a direct part of the RAF bombing offensive, completing fifty operations, including eight trips to Berlin, and earning himself the Distinguished Flying Cross.

I was never actually frightened. But the most awful experience, well – you'd be flying through the night and occasionally you would get anti-aircraft fire coming up. You would see the target from a long way off and fires had already started. You realized that the sky above it was filled with shell bursts – thousands. I thought, every time, how are we going to get through – you just couldn't see any way through. We were very lucky. We had bursts near us and shrapnel holes in the aircraft. You just accepted it – got on and did your job as you approached the target. I saw aircraft going down around us and that brought it home, but it's not going to happen to us, it's going to happen to someone else.

On a raid to Frankfurt a War Office correspondent joined John's crew. John was to aim his bombs at sky markers. 'I couldn't get a proper sight on these. They were floating about all over the place.' John told his pilot that they would have to go around again. 'We went over Frankfurt, all the way round and then back across our track. I was very concerned about dropping the bombs on a particular lot of flares.' John did so and 'then we got out. The crew were shouting all the time, "Get those bloody bombs going." I wasn't very popular!'

In January 1944, John and his crew were nearing completion of their first tour and they requested, and were granted, a transfer to No. 617 Squadron. Following further training on a new bombsight, the crew took part in numerous operations in support of the forthcoming D-Day beach landings in Normandy. On the day itself, following intensive training in the

preceding days, John took part in Operation 'Taxable', the dropping of Window (metallic strips) to the north-east of the actual invasion, deceiving German radar interpreters into believing this was another invasion fleet. Two days later John dropped his first 12,000lb Tallboy in the attack on the Saumur rail tunnel, and there followed a series of raids against the German secret weapon installations at Watten and Wizernes, with its distinctive concrete dome. On one of the raids on Wizernes John had his 'greatest success'.

I put my bomb right beside the dome – it shifted everything and a good thing I didn't hit the dome as it would probably have bounced off. You could follow the Tallboy all the way down and see it explode. I remember saying to my pilot, 'I've got a bull's eye.'

On 5 August John completed his fiftieth and final operation, attacking the U-boat pens at Brest.

John has been heavily involved in various fundraising initiatives for the Bomber Command Memorial.

66 *I thought it was pretty disgusting for Churchill not to have said something about the bombing after the war and to have just forgotten about Bomber Command. The political attitude was that we should have fought the war in a different way. Having taken part in it, you cannot believe that people would want to rewrite the war. It hurt that all those men died carrying out their job, their duty – that's what they volunteered to do and people didn't want to know anything about them after the war.*

For years Bomber Command carried the war to Germany and there were other aspects – it played a big part in the Battle of Britain and the Normandy invasion. But there has been no memorial. Bomber Command was brushed under the carpet.

The memorial has been a long time coming. I am very proud of the way the public has responded. At long last a chapter is closed and we have got recognition. Unfortunately, so many of us who survived are no longer here to see it. **99**

Designing Memory

The design brief given to Liam O'Connor when he was appointed as the architect in 2009 was simple: to create a memorial to honour the commitment, the sacrifice and the loss of 55,573 young lives in the service of their country. 'It wasn't an architectural brief,' said Liam. 'It was a case of "this is the problem, you are the architect, and you have to solve it".'

But even before Liam could sharpen his pencil to sketch out his first design, Westminster Council had set out its own criteria for what the monument must achieve. At a meeting in the council's offices in Victoria street in February 2009, Mike Gray, one of the council's planning officers, set out three key principles the council would expect to see in any design that was submitted. The first was that it must be of the highest quality, with long-lasting materials. Secondly, it must be properly landscaped, and thirdly it should be timeless, beautiful and discreet, without looking to the past for its ideas.

Mr Gray also made it clear that the memorial would come within the purview of the council's Public Art Advisory Panel, which expected to be consulted on any sculptures, statues, murals or other works of art on display in the borough. Liam O'Connor, aware of the council officer's preference for modernity, assured Mr Gray that any design he put forward would use traditional craftsmanship but would be indisputably 'modern and twenty-first century in character'. Like almost every other aspect of the memorial's story, that initial idea would change dramatically before the first stone would be laid.

One of the early ideas discussed during brainstorming sessions by the fledgling memorial committee was a wall with all 55,573 names inscribed on it, in Regent's Park. The BCA took the idea from memorials such as the Vietnam memorial in the USA, where families often touch the names of lost loved ones inscribed on it when they visit. That idea was dropped before Liam had been appointed, as the memorial committee quickly realized the cost of inscribing the names would be prohibitive (as well as problematic, with the potential elephant traps of getting a name wrong or missing someone off) as well as the location being too far from the centre of the capital.

Sir Michael Beetham was determined the memorial should be in central London, and Liam felt that Hyde Park Corner would be the best site, and submitted his first design drawings to the BCA. Aware of the preferences of the Public Art Advisory Panel, he put forward a design that would incorporate a contemporary bronze sculpture of an airman that he felt would appeal to the Art Panel's taste.

The memorial committee met at the Ministry of Defence to discuss the design. After a pregnant pause in which no one wanted to be the first to denounce it, the design was given a unanimous thumbs-down. Neither the veterans nor Jim Dooley or Robin Gibb wanted a contemporary sculpture, and Jim was given the task of breaking the news to Liam.

Over dinner in a Japanese restaurant in St James's in July 2009, Jim tactfully made it clear to Liam that a rethink was necessary. Liam was sympathetic to the veterans' wishes, but reiterated his belief that a traditional sculpture would be torpedoed by the Art Panel. 'Robin and I had always felt that the memorial had to be humanized,' said

Jim Dooley. 'We had looked at other war memorials, a lot of which were abstract, and we didn't want blobs of concrete or blobs of stone, we wanted a traditional, realistic representation of a bomber crew. From a very early stage a group of seven airmen, representing the crew of a typical heavy bomber, was top of our wish list, but we had no idea how much that would cost or how that might become a reality. In the end, a bronze of seven airmen was what we got, but it was a very roundabout route before we arrived there.'

Notwithstanding his belief that the Public Art Advisory Panel would prefer a contemporary sculpture, Liam came back to the memorial committee with an alternative design, a rotunda with four bronze panels telling the story of Bomber Command. An avenue of trees was to lead from it to a single effigy of an airman. The proposed location was in the centre of Green Park, as Sir Michael Beetham wanted visitors to appreciate the memorial in the tranquil heart of the park.

From the word go, Royal Parks, the administrator of the land, left no doubt that the scheme would not be supported if it was formally put forward. 'A memorial in this virgin part of the park was seen as an obstacle that couldn't be overcome,' said Liam. 'We sought to create a compromise; you cannot have a rotunda on the edge of a park, so we switched to a linear design. The eventual design was a riposte to the Ionic screen by Decimus Burton forming the gates to Hyde Park at Hyde Park Corner, making a picturesque symmetry; you come out of Hyde Park through one gate and into Green Park through another. The final design became the preferred choice in September 2009.'

But before any design could be accepted, the memorial committee was becoming nervous about just how much it might end up costing. Having never been involved in any remotely similar project, the veterans and trustees of the memorial had been forced to launch the appeal based on an educated guess of what the total bill would be. However, it was becoming clearer with each passing month that the original appeal target of £2 million had been a huge underestimate. But, as Liam O'Connor explained to the BCA, it was impossible to come up with a figure until a design had been agreed and fully costed by an independent quantity surveyor.

Liam submitted the approved design – by now Plan D – to Westminster Council at the end of 2009. The design was well

Page 62 Tony Iveson with the model of the Bomber Command Memorial. (Paul Grover) *Pages 64-65 and left* Architect's design illustration of the Bomber Command Memorial.

William Archibald

William was killed flying a No. 35 Squadron Handley Page Halifax, attacking the *Tirpitz* on the night of 30/31 March 1942. William is buried in Trondheim (Stavne) Cemetery, Norway.

received by Jim Dooley, Robin Gibb and Doug Radcliffe, all of whom felt it was exactly what they had envisaged all along. There were, however, other veterans who felt, with the modesty so typical of former bomber crewmen, that the proposed memorial was too big and should be scaled down. Liam argued strongly against this, and to help emphasize his point he took measurements of nearby buildings, including the Wellington Arch, the Decimus Burton screen and the Royal Artillery Memorial, believing the Bomber Command Memorial should echo the scale of them because it was 'commensurate with the importance' of its neighbours. The size of the memorial also had to reflect the vast number of lost lives that it was commemorating. 'Anything less than that, to me, would be an apology,' said Liam. He was adamant that the bold statement made by his new design was the right approach and would secure planning approval; to scale it down would be wrong.

Convinced by Liam's argument, the committee threw its weight behind this scheme, which went to the council's planning committee and gained consent in May 2010. Jim Dooley said: 'There are very few memorials where you can walk in and be a part of it. Most memorials you just observe from a distance, but with this design the public would be able to get inside it, and we anticipated it would become a popular thoroughfare for people entering Green Park, meaning it would give thousands of people pause for thought every year, even if they weren't making a specific visit to the memorial.'

As with any new building in a conservation area, planning consent came with conditions. Samples of stone and bronze would have to be submitted and, crucially, funds would have to be in place for its long-term maintenance before final consent could be granted. The design also had to address ecological elements, including the planting of twenty-five trees (a net gain of twelve over the thirteen that had to be cut down) and Liam O'Connor's design also included tube-shaped 'insect houses' in the roof and bat roosts (slots within the roof structure where bats can hang). In spring 2013 a wild flower meadow will be planted to attract insects and, in turn, bats.

The landscaping also includes a living relic of the final phase of the war in the shape of a yew tree that was originally planted in Potsdam, near Berlin, to commemorate the meeting in 1945 between Stalin, Churchill and Truman at which Germany's future was decided. The yew, which had fallen into neglect during the

Communist era, had been restored to health by an arboretum in Berlin, from which Jim Dooley and his brother Frank purchased it, so that it could be brought to London and planted at the western end of the memorial in the autumn of 2012.

One aspect of the design that evolved over time was the incorporation of 800lb of aluminium from the wreckage of a crashed Halifax bomber, which had been offered to the memorial team by Canadian crash recovery specialist Karl Kjarsgaard. LW682, part of No. 426 'Thunderbird' Squadron RCAF, was shot down in 1944, crashing into a swamp in Belgium with the loss of the seven Canadians and one Briton on board.

In 1997 Karl located the wreck and recovered the bodies of three of the Canadian airmen, who were given a full military funeral in Geraardsbergen, Belgium. The larger parts of the Halifax were sent to Canada to be used in the restoration of a Halifax at a museum in Trenton, Ontario, and aluminium parts that could not be used were melted down into ingots to be used for future air force memorials, plaques and statues. It was some of these ingots that Karl was offering for use in the Bomber Command Memorial. 'When Karl told me the story of where the ingots came from, I found the whole folklore around this very compelling,' said Liam. 'So I set myself the objective of finding a way of using it and came up with the idea of an aluminium ceiling. I wanted somehow to reflect the design of a Second World War bomber in the architecture. One of the ways of doing that would be to reflect the design of a fuselage. We spent a day at RAF Cosford with an expert, looking at a Wellington that was being worked on at the Sir Michael Beetham Conservation Centre. We took the contractors, and developed a design for the ceiling that paid homage to Barnes Wallis, the most outstanding designer of his generation.' The ceiling of the memorial would incorporate the famous geodetic lattice design of the Wellington airframe, with the aluminium fixed above it in riveted panels.

As Liam's design evolved, he was inspired by the eulogy read out at a memorial service to Barnes Wallis at St Paul's Cathedral. 'It was very moving,' said Liam. It read: 'But little in all his life pleased him quite as much as the knowledge that the magical ingenuity of his Wellington saved the lives of thousands of Commonwealth airmen and, from the most dramatic of all his war-time achievements came, not complacency, but promise for succeeding generations.'

September 1943–March 1944

Ferris Newton, of No. 76 Squadron, prepared for operations on 23 August 1943.

Our first raid on Berlin. We have heard such stories about the place – we are not at all happy about going there. I remember every one sitting around, out at the kite, waiting for start-up time, and nobody hardly speaking a word.

We are first wave in. Berlin is dotted with light – it is hard to distinguish the burst of anti-aircraft shells from the coloured markers dropped by the Pathfinders.

The first thing we have to do is fly through a wall of searchlights – hundreds, in cones and in clusters. A wall of light with very few breaks, and behind that wall an even fiercer light – glowing red and green and blue. Over that there are myriads of flares hanging in the sky. There is flak coming up at us now. All we see is a quick red glow from the ground and then up it comes on a level – a blinding flash. It's pretty obvious as we come in through the searchlight cones that it's going to be hell over the target.

There is one comfort and it's been a comfort to me all the time we have been going over – it is quite soundless. The roar of your engines drowns everything else. It's like running straight into the most gigantic display of soundless fireworks in the world. We are due over the target at 23.59; that's in about three minutes, and the bomb aimer is lying prone over his bomb sight, and the searchlights are coming nearer all the time. One cone splits and then it comes together again. They seem to splay out then stop, then come together again, and as they do there is a Lanc right in the centre. It's getting too hot with those searchlights, so we start weaving. George puts the nose down and we are pelting away at a furious rate. As we are coming out of the

searchlights more flak is coming up from the inner defence.

'Hullo Skipper.'

'Hullo Navigator.'

'Half a minute to go.'

'OK. Thanks for reminding me.'

'Keep weaving George, there is quite a lot of light stuff coming up as well – falling off a bit low.'

'Hullo Engineer. Will you put the revs up.'

'Engineer to Pilot. Revs up Skipper.'

'OK. Keep weaving George, a lot of searchlights and fighter flares, left.'

'Hullo Bomb Aimer. OK. Bomb doors open.'

'OK George – right – steady – a little bit longer yet OK – steady – right a little bit – right – steady – bombs still going – OK bombs gone. Keep weaving, there is some flak coming up. I can actually see ground detail skipper. Oh it's a wizard sight.'

'OK Andy. Don't get excited – keep your eyes open.'

'Engineer to Pilot. Jerry fighter just passed over the top of us – port to starboard.'

'OK Engineer. Keep your eyes open gunners.'

'Hullo Skipper. Will you turn onto zero 81.'

'Zero 81 right Navigator.'

'Engineer to Pilot. Another fighter crossing our course port to starboard.'

'OK Engineer.'

'There is a master searchlight probing for us George – keep weaving.'

Its beam swings past us, down goes the nose of the aircraft, the wings dip and we feel ourselves being flung about. We are swinging away, that master light is getting further and further away. We are out of it and now we are through

I turn and get a glimpse of that furious glowing carpet of light and explosions – that's all I can see of Berlin. We are beating out of it for home. The gunner's last sight of it is a great glow in the sky and around that glow a ring of searchlights, and all that's fifty miles away. We have only about another six hundred to do, but that last six hundred is covered in a much better spirit than the outward journey for everyone is light-hearted again.

The hours of darkness were going to get longer – they were going to prove deadly. Sir Arthur Harris decided it was time to send his crews, in force, to the 'black heart'. The destruction of Berlin, or the 'Big City' as crews called it, was Harris's aim, and he had no hesitation in launching the full weight of his Command into the offensive – to battle the growing enemy nightfighter force, to run the gauntlet of the deadly flak, to weave and dive away from the searchlights.

These would prove testing times for the aircrews of Bomber Command. No. 619 Squadron bomb aimer John Bell recalls:

At briefing they would pull back the curtain and you could see where you were going – red tape across the continent to the target, and then another tape for coming back. You knew what the target was immediately. In the early days of our operations it was, 'Oh, you know that sounds all right', it was a bit exciting – you didn't know what to expect. But as time went on there were gasps of 'Oh, not there again', particularly if it was to Berlin.

Canadian Alex Nethery served as a bomb aimer with Nos 427 and 405 Squadrons.

If there was one dreaded target that we hated to hear as our objective, it was Berlin! Goering once said that no Allied bomber would ever reach Berlin, and he pulled a lot of fighter squadrons and guns from other parts of Germany to defend the German capital. In addition to the heavy defences, this was a long trip – seven or eight hours – and practically every fighter station in Germany got a whack at you going over as well as coming back.

At the end of August and into early September Bomber Command had attacked Berlin on three nights, but results had been far from those achieved against Hamburg, with heavy losses. Harris paused, awaiting longer nights and advances in some of the Command's electronic navigational aids. Historians now regard the main 'Battle of

Left **Men of No. 77 Squadron based at RAF Elvington, Yorkshire, prior to their attack on Berlin during 30/31 January 1944.** *Below* **Crews of No. 199 Squadron are briefed in the station operations room at RAF Lakenheath, Suffolk, for a mine-laying sortie to be undertaken off the Dutch coast in March 1944.** (Air Historical Branch)

Right Lancaster captain, Flying Officer T. Blackburn, of No. 50 Squadron, keeps a firm hold on the crew's lucky mascot, as he is helped into his flying jacket by his flight engineer, Sergeant C. Walton, at RAF Skellingthorpe, on 19 February 1944. *Below* Sergeant H.C. Clayton, the bomb aimer of Handley Page Halifax, 'N-Nuts', of No. 77 Squadron, shows the crew's mascot, 'Wakee Wakee', to Air Commodore G. Walker, Air Officer Commanding No. 42 Base, at RAF Elvington, Yorkshire, in February 1944. On the left is the station commander of RAF Elvington, Group Captain S.S. Bertram, and to Clayton's immediate right are two pilots of No. 77 Squadron, Flight Lieutenant P.M. Cadman and Flight Lieutenant S.E. Wodehouse, both of whom were to lose their lives on bombing raids in June 1944. (Air Historical Branch)

Berlin' as opening on the night of 18/19 November 1943 and continuing until the end of January 1944 – comprising 14 main attacks, 7,403 sorties and the loss of 384 aircraft. But it was not just Berlin that received the attention of the RAF's heavies – that would have allowed the Germans to focus the defences. Other German targets also appeared in the bomb aimers' sights.

Sir Arthur Harris hoped the attacks would prove decisive. If nothing else the raids were firmly fixing the air battle over Germany. Enemy aircraft, 88mm guns and manpower were engaging the Bomber Boys, rather than being deployed against the Allied forces fighting in the Mediterranean, or the Russian forces on the Eastern Front.

In response, the German defences were strengthening and were adapting to the introduction of Window. And it must always be borne in mind that it was not always enemy action that resulted in a 'failed to return' being noted against aircraft in squadron records. The crews were always fighting with the weather conditions, the icing-up of their aircraft, or perhaps strong winds. Even if they had managed to survive flying over hostile territory, they would still have to land back safely at base, perhaps with damaged aircraft. Or maybe the weather conditions over the United Kingdom had deteriorated to such an extent that finding somewhere to land, anywhere to land, was a major feat, sometimes unachievable. One such example was the night of 16/17 December 1943, which came to be known as 'Black Thursday'. That night 483 Lancasters and 10 Mosquitoes were sent to attack Berlin and 25 aircraft were lost on the operation. However, those returning from the attack, having departed hostile skies and reached landfall on the English coast, faced extreme difficulty in finding somewhere, indeed anywhere, to land. Low cloud shrouded the air bases and, as fuel gauges showed that time was running out, aircrews became desperate. Some donned parachutes and abandoned their Lancasters. Other aircraft crashed as landings were attempted. As a consequence a further 29 Lancasters would later be scrubbed from squadron strengths – 148 men lost their lives, 39 were injured and 6 airmen would be recorded as lost at sea.

Through to March 1944 new operational records were broken, notably the loss rates. On the night of 19/20 February 1944 Bomber Command lost 78 aircraft on a deep penetration to Leipzig, the highest number failing to return on a single raid to date. Just over a month later 72 aircraft were either wrecked somewhere in occupied

Left The crew of a Short Stirling B.III of No. 622 Squadron report their experiences to an intelligence officer at RAF Mildenhall, Suffolk, after returning from the major raid on Berlin of 22/23 November 1943. *Right* Flying Officer A. E. Manning and his crew gather by their aircraft, Avro Lancaster B MkI, W4964 'WS-J', of No. 9 Squadron, shortly after their return to RAF Bardney, Lincolnshire, in the early hours of 6 January 1944, after raiding Stettin, Germany. (Air Historical Branch)

Europe, or were at the bottom of the North Sea – the costliest loss rate on a raid to Berlin, as Harris made one further attempt on the German capital. And then came the largest single loss of the entire war on the 30/31 March raid to Nuremberg. Ken Handley, who flew with No. 466 Squadron, wrote in his diary: 'Awe-inspiring at times & most certainly frightening & tense.' Almost 700 of Ken's colleagues were either dead or prisoners following the raid – 95 aircraft had failed to return.

Bomber Command's target list was, however – and perhaps fortunately in the light of recent losses – about to undergo a dramatic revision. The essential need to re-enter mainland western Europe became the overriding Allied demand on military manpower and resources. The actual seaborne and airborne invasion – D-Day, 6 June 1944 – was still some months off. Yet Bomber Command would be tasked with softening Hitler's Atlantic Wall and blasting a ring around the prospective battle zone to hinder German reinforcement.

Teddy Burrell

Royal Air Force

Air Gunner

Teddy Burrell married May Jones on 7 July 1941. On 15 July 1942 their daughter Valerie was born. In the meantime and unbeknown to May, Teddy had written, but not sent, a letter.

Croft
2nd May 1942

Dearest,

It's now about 7pm, & I have about three hours to wait before I do a spot of night-flying training, so I thought I'd try & do a bit of explaining to you.

When you read this letter one of two things will have probably happened. Either I shall be home & off 'operations' or I shall be 'missing'. That is why I want to write this letter Dearest.

I think I had better start from the beginning but if this seems a bit confused forgive me because it seems awkward to explain myself.

Well to start with as you know, I gave up a comparatively safe & progressive ground job to become an air gunner. I could have got out of it but I hadn't the 'guts'. Some people may

think I'm a fool but I believed that by flying I could perhaps help in a very small way to bringing this awful war to a quicker close. I believed also that by marrying you I was given the right to protect you & could do this by helping, again in my own small way, in actually fighting in this war. Well my darling, you know how I became an air gunner & how I went to Ireland on Defiant night fighters. As far as operational flying went this was pretty safe & I considered myself lucky. I was satisfied too that at last I was doing something, although not much compared with others. Then the squadron started to lose their Defiants and air gunners were no longer needed. I tried with the rest of the chaps to become a Radio Observer but the Air Ministry said no, so after about three weeks wasted training we were all posted. Two of us eventually arrived here at Croft.

Now this is where I have to confess to deceiving you Darling. I've never done it before & I hope I never have to do it again. I hope you understand that I had to & I couldn't help it. I wrote to you when I arrived here & said that apart from a few normal changes this station was the same & I couldn't understand why I had been posted. That was wrong as I have already explained why I was posted. The main thing was that I didn't say what aircraft I was to fly in. Well they were big four-engine Halifaxes. Understand Darling, I was to fly over Germany of a night & also sometimes of a day. It was the one thing you dreaded wasn't it? That's the reason why I didn't tell you. I hadn't the heart Darling I love you too much. At the moment there are only two months to go before our baby

comes into this world & I don't think that it would do you any good, your health, to know what I was doing & to worry as I know you would. I believe that for this once that what the mind doesn't know the heart doesn't grieve. You do understand and forgive me Dearest don't you? If anything does happen to me you will know & I think that will be soon enough.

Again I could have got out of flying but again I hadn't the 'guts'. If I had refused to fly I would not be a Sgt long but that didn't worry me. The thing that did was the fact that I would be branded as yellow & I couldn't stand that. You see my point Darling? What could I do? As far as I could see I could do nothing except hope I got away OK.

I've got 30 trips to do which at the present rate should only take about three months. I shan't start for about a month as I have to get used to the new aircraft. Taking into consideration all this & hoping nothing extraordinary happens, I should be off flying about September. This is only a rough guess though. After my 30 trips I shall become an instructor & I shall not be called on to fly on operations again. 30 trips may sound a lot but it's not really. There are hundreds of chaps that have done 30 trips & volunteered for more. It's just luck & I am praying I have good luck, not for myself but for your sake. I don't ever want you to be unhappy Darling.

If you do happen to get this letter in unhappy circumstances, which I pray to God you won't, remember Darling unhappy moments often turn into happy ones. Never give up hope. There are hundreds who become prisoners & are not "found" for months and months. Don't give up hope until after the war when you can be certain. Keep your chin up, take care of yourself and always keep smiling. Let the world see that smile that I love so much. Whatever happens I shall remember you with your smile Beloved & it's a wonderful & sweet memory. Have faith in God my Darling & remember I've always loved you dearly & always will. You are my most precious possession & I wish I could take care of you as I would like to, but that will have to wait until this war is over.

Well Darling I think this is about all. I haven't told anyone yet but I think I will tell Cis and give her this letter

to give to you. I'm not writing to mum. I would like you to explain to her if you will Darling.

I am afraid this letter is a bit confused but I keep thinking of you & can't help it. I hope I haven't missed anything, I don't think so.

Well Darling, to close I want to wish you every happiness for ever & I hope I can give you all of it.

I love you my Dearest more than anything in the world. Remember, don't give up hope & keep your chin up Darling. 'Au revoir', not Goodbye Beloved.
Yours with all my Love
My Dearest
Teddy

On the night of 11/12 August 1942 Teddy Burrell's No. 78 Squadron Halifax failed to return from a raid to Mainz. Teddy was killed, along with four other members of his crew, and they were buried in Méan Communal Cemetery, Belgium. May Burrell, subsequently, received Teddy's letter of 2 May 1942.

Gordon Mellor

Royal Air Force

Navigator

O**n the morning** of 5 October 1942, at RAF Elsham Wolds, No. 103 Squadron navigator Gordon Mellor awoke to the sound of distant thunder. Ops were on and Gordon's crew were detailed to fly their Handley Page Halifax to Aachen that night, but, because of the weather, 'we rather thought ops were going to be scrubbed'.

The Met. Officer said we would get a few bumps and the air was quite unstable – rather rough weather for quite a way, though we would possibly have it clear over the target. Everyone gave him a rousing cheer. It was part of the build-up.

We had the final meal, got kitted out and waited to be taken to the aircraft. In the Halifax normal checks were carried out and off we went. We were routed southerly to go across the English Channel just east of London, then a turning point in France and a straight run to Aachen. Suddenly, over Belgium, the weather cleared. It was a brilliant night and we saw a magical display of the Northern Lights.

We saw activity either side of us – one or two planes went down. There were fighters about.

Gordon directed his crew to the target, bombs were dropped, and course was set for home.

We had gone in at about 12,000 feet and by the time we came out we were down to 10,000 feet. We were trying to avoid the light flak beneath us and the heavier flak that went up to about 15,000 feet – flying between the two. Four or five minutes out of the target area the rear gunner called out: 'There is a fighter behind us. It's a Me110. He's sitting there shadowing us.' We had a conference over the intercom. A general discussion followed and it was the pilot's decision finally, we would try and scare him off. The rear gunner and mid-upper gunner let fly. The nightfighter was 500 yards or so back, rather a long way for a .303 machine gun. The nightfighter pulled in a bit closer and started pumping cannon shell at us, causing damage and hitting the rear gunner. There were two further attacks. He was no beginner, he knew what he was doing, and the inboard engines on both sides were set on fire. You could see the tracer whizzing past. None of us in the front of the aircraft was hit. Neither was the mid-upper gunner, so it was the poor rear gunner who took the packet.

We were beginning to lose power, the wings and the inboard engines were in flames, and we were going down at quite a rate. We were twisting and turning – whatever the pilot could do to try and avoid the attacks.

The Me110 disappeared from our view. We were getting quite low. Our speed had been terrific on the down gradient. The pilot said everybody out – abandon aircraft. The escape hatch was right underneath my seat, which I whisked away.

The trap door was pulled up, and by that time Gordon had been joined by the front gunner and the wireless operator.

We passed the main pilot's parachute up and then it was time to be out – he said 'Come on, hurry up.' I got my parachute on, swung my legs out over the opening and was dropping my bottom on to the edge when I felt a shove on my shoulders. I was gone. The slipstream caught me. I slid underneath, more

or less horizontal, and the tail of the plane passed over. That was the last I saw of it. I was supposed to count to 10 but having seen the tail plane go I thought the parachute was not going to foul, so I pulled the ripcord.

I came to a sudden sort of rest. The parachute was tight – quite a jolt in the nether regions. I didn't see what happened to the aircraft. I tried to swing round but by that time I was in the tops of trees. I was very lucky. I stayed there swinging in the trees for a couple of minutes, to gather my senses. I thought, 'Right I've got to get down. I've got to hide the parachute.' I pressed the knob on the box where the parachute harnesses joined. They fell apart, the harness virtually fell off, and I fell. It was all of 12 inches at the most. I was fine. The only problem was the parachute in the tree.

Unable to retrieve his parachute, and with dogs barking, Gordon moved off. From Gordon's crew of eight that night, three men lost their lives and the four others were captured. Gordon eventually found help and was passed along various evasion lines through Holland, Belgium, and France, then across the Pyrenees to Spain, before returning to the UK. On 1 November, on Gordon's birthday, he arrived back at his home in Wembley, London.

❝ *The memorial recognizes the input of the youth of our country and our Allies in times of emergency. It is a symbol not only of the casualties, which were very high, but of all who took part. The war was thrust upon them. They didn't have a say in it. At the end of the war the armchair people came out and were quite derogatory about the effort of Bomber Command. The balance is being put right.* ❞

Veterans in Portrait
John Banfield MBE

Royal Air Force

Wireless Operator/Air Gunner

and Bomb Aimer

The awful cost of war became terribly apparent to Londoner John Banfield as his training progressed prior to joining an operational bomber squadron. John had been inspired to take to the air when, as a young boy, he had watched in awe as the pre-war aviators took to the skies at Croydon and Biggin Hill. In June 1940 John embarked upon his RAF training, destined to become a wireless operator/air gunner and then a bomb aimer with RAF Bomber Command. But, if John did have any notions of romanticizing the act of war, they were quickly dispelled while at No. 14 Operational Training Unit RAF Cottesmore. On three separate occasions John took the responsibility of being a pall-bearer. As John recalled, 'The previous course got practically wiped out.'

John carried out his first operation on 22 January 1942, flying a No. 207 Squadron Avro Manchester. Then through 1942, having converted on to Avro Lancasters, John would take part in a further twenty-three operations, including the first thousand-bomber raid to Cologne, recalling, 'before we crossed the Dutch coast we could see Cologne on fire', and an attack on Bremen on 29 June, 'we were caught in a heavy ack-ack barrage with shrapnel damage to the fuselage'. Midway through John retrained for bomb-aiming duties. Three days into his new training his first crew failed to return, with a total loss of life. 'The fact that I remustered saved my life.'

John's flying logbook records the basic facts of his Bomber Command operations: date, hour, aircraft type and no., pilot, duty, remarks, flying time. Following a raid in May, John penned: '29.5.42, 22.00–04.40, Lancaster 5628-Q, F/Sgt McCarthy, 2nd W/op & AG, "Operation" Mining the Sound at Copenhagen (a/c shot up rear gunner wounded), 6.40.' Behind every simplistic summary inked into the regimented columns of John's logbook a terrible, tragic, perhaps heroic, perhaps pitiful, perhaps horrific human drama had unfolded. On the operations John flew on during 1942, 195 aircraft failed to return, the vast majority of each of these aircraft carrying seven airmen. A simple statistical calculation, using the loss statistics suffered by Bomber Command on John's operations, shows, exactly, that he had a one in three chance of survival. John's response to such statistics echoes a familiar reaction from Bomber Command veterans. 'I was very lucky.'

But John's good fortune would finally run out on his first operation of 1943, the night of 3/4 January, when the gunfire from a German nightfighter raked his aircraft, and set an engine on fire. The order came to bale out, but the situation became progressively desperate. The hatch in the nose would not budge, and the path back down the fuselage was blocked by a flaring petrol line. John then saw his navigator launch himself through the side of the Lancaster, where the Perspex blister had been blasted away.

'Bloody Hell,' I thought, 'the inboard motor propeller is within a foot of that.' I looked out and could see that the flight

engineer, who was OK when I got out, had feathered the inboard motor. The petrol behind it was on fire. I saw the navigator get clear so I followed suit. We were going near on 200 m.p.h. and the slipstream caught me. I was swept round. My chute was inside the aircraft and I was outside. I heaved myself back inside to get my chute, tagged it to my chest and went under the mainplane, striking the tail unit with my shoulder.

John lost consciousness, but when he came to he was swinging, suspended by his parachute, caught in a tree. Shortly after John was released by some German airmen, taken to a nearby airfield, where he received immediate medical aid, and then on to a hospital in Amsterdam. For four weeks John underwent treatment. 'I wouldn't have been medically treated better had the same thing happened in England.' John eventually ended up at Stalag VIIIB at Lamsdorf, seeing out the war from the wrong side of barbed wire.

66 *If it hadn't been for Bomber Command, the Germans would have been over here. The loss we suffered: nearly half the chaps who volunteered for aircrew duties in the war lost their lives.* **99**

'Don't forget to bring your sandwiches.'

Berlin
23/24.8.1943

Berlin. 23 August 1943. The German capital. The comparative still of the night is disrupted by the first wail of the air-raid sirens. More than 700 aircraft are at that very moment heading that way. Many Berliners are disbelieving and choose not to take to their shelters. It is a decision that will lead to an unusually high number of civilian casualties.

Harris has been waiting for this moment for many months. The nights are getting longer. His squadrons are better equipped. His men are ready. The tonnage of bombs he is able to deliver is unprecedented.

There are factors against him, however. Oboe, the secret bombing device, does not have sufficient range to be used on Berlin. H2S, his other navigational 'joker in the pack', is not best suited to heavily built-up areas. The contrast between land and water provides a better 'picture' on the device's cathode ray screen. The German nightfighter force is in the ascendancy and gaining in confidence and victories, and the distance to Berlin – a seven-hour round trip of more than 1,200 miles – means more fuel and fewer bombs are carried. But Harris is determined. The weather is on their side. The codeword – Whitebait – has been issued. Operations are 'on'.

The route to the target is virtually direct, crossing the Dutch coast and with only a slight detour to avoid the defences at Bremen, Hanover, Brunswick, and Magdeburg. The bombers will in fact fly slightly beyond Berlin, and then turn back over the target to approach from the south. The idea is to kick down the back door. At the vanguard are the Pathfinders, the corps d'élite of Bomber Command, led by a Canadian Master Bomber, Wing Commander Johnnie Fauquier, the officer commanding No. 405 Squadron.

Fauquier is not the most senior officer flying that night, however. Three station commanders (Group Captains Alfred Willetts, Basil Robinson, and Noel Fresson from Oakington, Graveley, and Bourn respectively) have also opted to fly, conscious perhaps of the significance of this – the first major attack on Berlin – and the importance of leading from the front. Willetts's captain, Squadron Leader Charles Lofthouse, welcomes his CO with a smile: 'Don't forget to bring your sandwiches for the trip home, sir.'

Perhaps inevitably, there are problems. Pathfinder navigators struggle to identify the centre of Berlin from the indistinct patterns on their H2S screens, and the marking is awry. Main Force is late, and several crews decide to cut corners to make up time. A great many bombs fall in open countryside, or on the southern suburbs of the city. But not every bomb is wasted. A good many industrial buildings are hit, in what will later be described by the Berlin authorities themselves as the most serious raid of the war so far.

The damage inflicted, however, is not without heavy cost. Although the stream is unmolested on its way into the target, the illusion of peace is quickly shattered once the German controllers finally order all their fighters to concentrate on Berlin. Radar-controlled 'Tame Boar' fighters and their freelancing, single-engined 'Wild Boar' colleagues are quickly on the scene, and into the fray. Suddenly the sky is lit up with searchlights and tracer. Charles Lofthouse looks out from his cockpit to see his port outer engine on fire, and a deep blue flame spreading rapidly. He orders his crew – and his distinguished passenger – to take to their chutes, and remembers the Group Captain disappearing 'like a rat out of a trap'.

A Halifax of No. 158 Squadron is on its bombing run, when the air bomber, Dennis Slack, sees two lines of tracer and hears a series of rapid explosions somewhere to the rear. On his skipper's orders, he puts on his parachute and bales out: 'I dropped away and as I did so the port wing, which was a mass of flames, swung up and the plane went into a steep dive, taking the skipper with it. He never got out.'

By the end of the night, some fifty-six Lancasters, Halifaxes, and Stirlings have been shot down – Bomber Command's greatest loss in a single night up to that point in the war. There are further losses in collisions and when an aircraft blows up before take-off. Two out of the three station commanders are missing. As well as Willetts, the much-decorated Basil Robinson is also lost, killed in action, and crews at his home base are stunned by his loss. The nightfighters do not have it all their own way, however, and the air gunners fight back. Five Bf110s and six Fw190s and Bf109s are shot down, and a further seven aircraft damaged by their own flak, such are the risks taken in what would ultimately become an unequal struggle.

This is the first in a new major battle – the Battle of Berlin – that will comprise a further eighteen raids until the assault finally ends on 31 March 1944, when new targets are found to support the invasion. There are no winners. Bomber Command loses 625 aircraft and crews, and at least a further 80 will crash in Britain with heavy loss of life. And Bomber Command does not only attack Berlin during this period. It also executes a further thirty-six major raids against other important German industrial targets, and takes further casualties. Morale is sorely tested. To survive a tour of operations in the winter of 1943–44 takes every ounce of skill, nerve, and luck that the crews can muster. The Bomber Boys will remember other targets, but they will never forget Berlin.

Right A WAAF intelligence officer, Section Officer P. Duncalfe, questions Warrant Officer H. Blunt, the pilot of a No. 49 Squadron Avro Lancaster B.III, JB362/EA-D, on the crew's return to RAF Fiskerton, Lincolnshire, from a raid on Berlin on 22/23 November 1943. On their next sortie to Berlin, five days later, Blunt and his crew were shot down in 'D-Donald' and killed. (Air Historical Branch)

Veterans in Portrait
Harry Irons DFC

Royal Air Force

Air Gunner

Harry Irons completed the extraordinary total of sixty bombing operations with RAF Bomber Command – with No. 9 Squadron on Lancasters and then with No. 158 Squadron on Halifaxes. In September 1942, Harry, still a teenager, carried out his first operation over enemy territory.

Stubbs, our skipper, said to me, 'You're going in the mid-upper turret for a few trips to get acclimatized to what's going on and then you can change over and become the rear gunner.' I said, 'That's fair enough.' Before we went to briefing we had a night flying test, half-hour trip. We tested the guns, the bomb aimer tested the sight, the engineer tested the engines. When we landed, the bomber aimer (an old sweat of about 26; we called him the 'old boy'), said, 'We're going to Happy Valley tonight. You can tell by the bomb load, one 4,000 pounder and 1,200 incendiaries.'

We got ourselves ready, sat, wrote letters, and then went for briefing. All of a sudden the CO would come in and we would all have to stand up. We were a scruffy lot really, just had

battledress on. Some had ties, some scarfs. There was a big sheet over a board. They pulled it off and there it was, Düsseldorf. The bomb aimer said, 'I told you it was going to be Happy Valley.' I thought, 'Well that doesn't sound too bad, Happy Valley.'

We went to have some grub, bacon and eggs. Then we got escape kit, a few sweets, a little box with foreign currencies in it, a little water bag and some tablets you could put in to kill all the germs, a flask of coffee if you wanted it. Then down to the crew room to dress. It was quiet, just like a morgue, nobody laughing or joking, everybody looking at each other. All very serious. Put on your silk underwear, long johns, then top, uniform, electrical heated suit, flying jacket and leather fur

trousers. Zip 'em all up, scarf on. A WAAF would come round, put us on a lorry and take us to the aircraft. We sat about talking, everybody smoked except the pilot. He never drunk, he never went out with women, he never swore. Although the strange thing was that, when we got airborne, Stubbs's language … I could not believe the language right till we got back.

We took off for Düsseldorf. I was excited. In that mid-upper you could see everything, up, down, look around, brilliant vision. We got to the Dutch coast, flying about 12,000–14,000 feet. I could see this flak below us. I didn't realize what it was, every colour you could think of was coming up. It looked so beautiful from a distance, slowly coming up, slowly coming up, slowly coming up. But it didn't come up as high as us, because it was only light flak. We climbed up to about 19,000 feet and went across Holland. The bomb aimer said, 'target ahead'. I swung my turret round and I had the fright of my life. I could not believe what I saw. Honestly. I could not believe what I saw; the amount of shells and ex-plosions in the distance. I thought to myself we've got to go through this. I couldn't believe it. As we got over the target, the bomb aimer said, 'I've missed the target skipper. We've got to go round again.' I couldn't believe it. We made a U-turn, went right round and came in again. They were knocking the hell out of us. I thought to myself 'dear oh dear'. Anyway, we came back. I remember a couple of the crew had trouble with their oxygen, so the skipper said, we'll have to go down to below 10,000 feet. As we hit the Dutch coast, this lovely coloured stuff was coming up at us, shooting past us. How it never hit us I don't know, hundreds of these shells belting past us. We got back all right, but with quite a few holes in the aircraft. I did say to the skipper, 'Oh that flak!' He said, 'It's OK, you'll get used to it.' Well you never got used to it. In fact it got worse and worse and worse. How a plane could fly through that flak I don't know and yet very very few bomber crews refused to go. Very few said no we've had enough. There were a few, but most of them carried on, and they knew they weren't going to finish a tour.

When we got back, we'd go into the briefing room, have a

cup of coffee. They'd ask us what went on, if we had seen any fighters. At that period the fighter menace wasn't as bad as it was later on. But the flak – deadly. I've seen time and time again an aircraft going in and just one shell – bang! Just like that, especially if they had got the bomb load on. Sometimes you would see bombs hitting another aircraft below. The most amazing thing, I can never make out, is how they got 200–300 bombers in that target area in such a little while. A lot used to weave about, couldn't help it, try and get out of the search-lights. Not only did you have to watch the fighters and the flak, you had to watch the bombs, somebody coming in front of you, underneath you. It was absolutely horrendous.

" We have been hoping for this memorial for years and years. I am pleased that we made a determined effort and I am very proud to be one of the people responsible for it. It is a wonderful tribute and it should have happened after the war. **"**

Becoming Reality

David's No. 83 Squadron Avro Lancaster fell to earth during a raid to Düsseldorf on the night of 31 December 1942/1 January 1943. David is buried, as is his entire crew, in Uden War Cemetery, Netherlands.

The foundation stone of the memorial was laid by HRH The Duke of Gloucester in a ceremony in Green Park on 4 May 2011.

On a gloriously sunny spring day, the Venerable (Air Vice-Marshal) Ray Pentland, Chaplain-in-Chief of the RAF, conducted a service that included a reading by Chief of the Air Staff, Air Chief Marshal Sir Stephen Dalton. The Duke then laid a symbolic pat of mortar on top of the stone with a shiny new trowel, and to complete the ceremony the BBMF's Lancaster flew overhead to add its own tribute.

Veterans including Sir Michael Beetham, Tony Iveson and Doug Radcliffe were joined by Robin Gibb, John Caudwell and Lord Ashcroft to see the stone 'laid'. In fact, the stone was some distance from the actual site of the memorial, as conditions attached to the planning consent had not yet been fulfilled, so work had not begun. It would be almost another four months before the issue of the covenant to pay for the memorial's upkeep would finally be settled, triggering full planning consent.

Work finally began on the site on 29 August 2011, starting with the felling of thirteen trees that had to come down to make way for the memorial (a total of twenty-five trees would be planted in their place, giving the park a net gain of twelve).

Even before the foundations could be dug, however, the first costly snag of the building process had to be overcome. Liam O'Connor had discovered that a gas pipe supplying much of Mayfair ran underneath the site and had to be moved, which would have

added £80,000 to the cost had it not been for the generosity of National Grid, which diverted the pipe and donated £50,000 towards the cost.

Meanwhile, the stone for the memorial was already being quarried at Jordans quarry on the isle of Portland in Dorset. Almost 1,000 tons of Portland stone was blasted out of the ground, all of which had to be shipped to master stonemasons S. McConnell & Sons in Kilkeel, County Down. Every stone had to be designed by Liam O'Connor's staff, who sent the measurements, angles and curves to Ireland to be machined and hand-finished with millimetre-perfect precision. For the memorial to be completed before the

London 2012 Olympics, when all building work in the capital had to cease, McConnell's had to work twenty-four hours a day, six days a week, for six months. When the stones were shipped back to England, project managers working out of portable cabins on the site in Green Park used colour-coded draughtsman's drawings pinned on the walls to make sure every stone went in its predetermined place, like a giant Lego model.

Even the lime mortar for the joints between the stones had to be designed specially for the project. Bob Bennett MBE, from The Lime Centre in Hampshire, worked with Liam to design a mix of the right aggregates and mortar made in a time-honoured way to stay in keeping with the other buildings in the area and to match the colour of the stone. 'There weren't many problems with the build once we got going,' said Liam. 'We had to condemn some stones because they had cracks in them and they had to be remade, but it's not the errors that are important, it's how you react to them.'

One of the workers on the site did a twenty-seven-hour journey just to get two stones to the site. The build was on hold because they were very large stones critical to the east wing. The builder drove all the way to Ireland and all the way back, and got stopped by the police when he was two miles from the memorial site because they suspected the van was overladen. When he explained to the police what he was doing, they gave him an escort all the way to the site. The stones were laid within an hour of him getting there.

Around thirty staff from the builders in charge of the memorial, Gilbert-Ash Ltd, from Northern Ireland, were on site on an average day, but between 300 and 400 people worked on the monument all told, including stonemasons, quarrymen, foundry workers, architects, landscape gardeners and, of course, the sculptor.

By the time the final design had been agreed, the memorial was to be a truly international venture, with materials and labour coming from as far afield as Canada, Australia, Norway and Germany. Both Liam and the memorial committee had been eager to involve Commonwealth and Allied nations in contributing to the finished building, to recognize the high proportion of Bomber Command casualties from countries other than Britain.

Colin Dudley DFC was one of around 10,000 Australians who served in Bomber Command, navigating Halifaxes with No. 578

Page 84 **Robin Gibb visits the Bomber Command Memorial site in February 2012.** (Mark Kehoe via the *Daily Express*); *Page 85* **The laying of the foundation stone on 4 May 2011, with architect Liam O'Connor far left.** (Paul Grover) *Left* **The Battle of Britain Memorial Flight's Lancaster conducts a flypast at the laying of the memorial foundation stone.** (Paul Grover) *Right* **Lord Ashcroft at the Bomber Command Memorial site in May 2012.** (*Daily Express*)

Squadron and completing thirty-nine sorties, then turning to sculpture after the war. He contacted the BCA offering to sculpt a bronze wreath that could be a focal point for future services of remembrance, and the BCA gratefully accepted. The wreath was by far the largest sculpture he had ever undertaken and, after months of painstaking work at his home in Adelaide, it was flown to the Middle East by the Royal Australian Air Force, then brought to England by an RAF C17 transport aircraft, before being flown on by a Chinook to the RAF Museum, where it went on display in the Bomber Hall from April 2012 until it was installed on the memorial itself. Liam described the wreath as 'a masterful work in bronze that makes a profound and symbolic contribution to the memorial'.

On the other side of the world, Karl Kjarsgaard's aluminium ingots from the crashed Halifax, weighing 800lb, had been transported from Canada to Britain by the Royal Canadian Air Force and then onward to Norway, via Grimsby, for smelting. Sean Kelly from Richard Austin Alloys had contacted Norsk Hydro in Norway and Gilmour Metals in Glasgow, who offered to give their services for free. The ingots were smelted into sheets 2mm thick (which is a lot thicker than the fuselage of a Second World War aircraft) and the sheets were shipped back to Gilmour's, which did further work in preparing the aluminium. The struts for the stainless steel structure, echoing the geodesic design of the Wellington, were made by Littlehampton Welding in East Sussex. Then Dave Martin Roofing Ltd fixed it all together, with copper sheets covering the weather side of the roof.

Stone engraver Richard Kindersley carved the inscriptions using the traditional hammer and chisel method, with a unique typeface he designed himself for the memorial, using letters that 'fly' upwards to reflect the subject of the monument. Around the edge of the roof opening is the RAF's motto *Per Ardua Ad Astra*, while the inside walls of the memorial bear Churchill's famous words about Bomber Command: 'The fighters are our salvation but the bombers alone provide the means of victory.' Facing Churchill's quotation is a simple inscription which reads: 'This memorial is dedicated to the 55,573 airmen from the United Kingdom British Commonwealth & allied nations who served in RAF Bomber Command & lost their lives over the course of the Second World War.' As an acknowledgement of the civilians who were killed by bombs dropped from both sides during the war, the memorial bears the words: 'This memorial also commemorates those of all nations who lost their lives in the bombing of 1939–1945.' The plinth supporting the sculpture, faced in red granite, is inscribed with part of the oration from the funeral of the Ancient Greek leader Pericles: 'Freedom is the sure possession of those alone who have the courage to defend it.'

Churchill's words had summed up Bomber Command's contribution to Allied victory, while Sir Michael Beetham, who chose the quotation from the funeral of Pericles after discussions with Doug Radcliffe and Sebastian Cox of the Air Historical Branch, had always felt the sentiment expressed 2,500 years ago captured the essence of the courage of men who flew over occupied Europe knowing they faced worse odds than even infantry officers in the First World War.

In all, the memorial cost £4.1 million to build, with another £1 million for the sculpture, the remainder of the cost going on professional fees and legal bills. On 24 April 2012, John Caudwell, the biggest single benefactor and the nephew of a Bomber Boy, was given the honour of laying the final stone, atop one of the columns on the east wing. It is inscribed with the words: 'This last stone was laid by John Caudwell principal benefactor of this memorial.'

Left On 20 March 2012 the bronze wreath sculptured by Colin Dudley DFC arrives by Chinook at the RAF Museum, Hendon. Left to right – Flight Lieutenant Graeme Court (99 Squadron), Flight Lieutenant J. J. Gooding (18 'B' Squadron), Squadron Leader Glenn Cole (18 'B' Squadron), Master AV Loadmaster Andy Gillett (18 'B' Squadron), Squadron Leader Pez Coles (18 'B' Squadron), RAAF Wing Commander Peter Miller. (Jonathan Buckmaster via the *Daily Express*) *Right* John Caudwell at the Bomber Command Memorial site. (Steve Reigate via the *Daily Express*)

William Meager

William lost his life on a No. 463 (RAAF) Squadron Avro Lancaster attacking Darmstadt on the night of 11/12 September 1944. Bill is buried in Dürnbach War Cemetery, Germany.

Bomber Command at War

April 1944–August 1944

General Sir Bernard Montgomery was clear with his 'musts' – the imperatives for the successful re-entry of Allied troops to western Europe in the summer of 1944. At St Paul's School, Hammersmith, London, on 15 May 1944, Montgomery, in command of the Allied ground forces for the forthcoming invasion, was unequivocal about the input he required from his naval and air force colleagues, as part of the Operation 'Overlord' plan.

We must blast our way ashore and get a good lodgement before the enemy can bring sufficient reserves up to turn us out. . . . We must gain space rapidly, and peg out claims inland. And while we are engaged in doing this, the air must hold the ring and must hinder and make very difficult the movement of enemy reserves by train or road.

And the 'musts' held the day, with the RAF's heavy bomber forces committing fully and prioritizing support to the forthcoming assault on the Normandy beaches. Indeed, this imperative came as no surprise to the airmen, as they had actually been involved in establishing the 'ring' for the ten weeks prior to the St Paul's meeting. RAF Bomber Command had attacked the Trappes railyards on the night of 6/7 March, the first in an extensive series of raids against the rail targets in northern France and Belgium, through which German troops and armour would deploy to the proposed Normandy battle area. Bomber Command would also attack radar stations and coastal gun batteries, bombard enemy troop concentrations and barracks, make supply drops to the French Resistance, and carry out decep-

tion raids in the run-up to D-Day and beyond. Essential to the success of the raids was accuracy. Sir Arthur Harris remained aware of the limitations of his Command and the weaponry when it came to accuracy, and fearful of friendly civilian casualties, yet the attacks were deemed military necessities.

On 8 March 1944 Sir Arthur Harris sent a dispatch stating that raids on 'lightly defended targets' in France were 'practically nil', and 'no way comparable to those associated with long-range targets in Germany'. So as to avoid some aircrews experiencing 'far less risk and strain than others', and with the planned escalation in the number of attacks on targets in France and the occupied territories and the probable high turnaround of crews because of the thirty-operation tour limit, Harris decided to differentiate and classed these 'lightly defended' raids as counting as only one-third of a sortie. Unsurprisingly this was not met with general approval by the aircrews. Canadian air gunner John 'Jack' Fitzgerald wrote home on 18 May commenting on raids to France and complaining that 'each trip consists of only 1/3 of an op., which is silly, because if you go over there and get killed you don't get only 1/3 killed'. (Jack would lose his life on a mine-laying raid in August 1944.)

Bill Geeson, a pilot with No. 625 Squadron, provides a case in point. He flew to Mailly-le-Camp on 3/4 May 1944, a night on which forty-two Lancasters were lost. He recalled: 'It was quite horrific.'

They told us, 'Oh it's easy, you know. You've only got to go to France.' But it was a bad one. There was low cloud and a bright moon, the very things that we didn't want. We saw aircraft being shot down and one in particular

my feelings about bombing were of great satisfaction, as I felt that I was directly helping to protect my family.' Bomber Command would also, at this stage, return to daylight operations in force – for many a new experience. American Rick Green, a navigator with No. 44 Squadron, was on a raid to a flying-bomb target in August 1944, and heard his rear gunner call out over the intercom, 'Oh, the poor bastards.' 'What happened?' Rick asked. 'The bomb from a plane up above tore off the wings of another Lanc' came the reply from his crewmate. Norman Turton served with No. 207 Squadron and similarly recalled a tragic incident on a daylight raid to a flying-bomb target in August.

As navigator, when I got near the target I used to put on paper my courses out of the target and then go and stand up at the front. With this being daylight, I could see aircraft all above us, and there were bombs coming down like leaflets. I thought, 'bloody hell'. There was an aircraft at the side of us that just disintegrated. It was there one second and at the blink of an eye-lid it was gone.

One of the most significant V-1 targets attacked by the Bomber Boys was the cave system at Saint-Leu d'Esserent – a storage depot for the flying bombs. These raids substantially lowered the V-1 launch rates, but at a cost: 13 aircraft on 4/5 July and 31 aircraft three nights later. Russell Gradwell, a pilot with No. 9 Squadron, flew to Saint-Leu d'Esserent on 7/8 July 1944:

The nightfighters were queuing up waiting for us when we crossed the French coast. Fights broke out all around us and we were lucky nobody bothered us until we got about halfway towards the target. Then a nightfighter closed in on us . . . I think that one of the gunners luckily got a hit on the fighter and knocked the pilot out, because I was corkscrewing and the gunner suddenly screamed to me 'level out', which I did and the nightfighter passed just underneath us.

Russell's crew carried on to the target, at which point he realized that 'we had a wing on fire'. As soon as they had bombed, the crew tried to put the fire out. 'We couldn't do it. We tried everything. We switched all the fuel off on the port side and shut both engines down.' Russell's flight engineer, realizing the aircraft was doomed,

which was rather unusual, was a bomber, which was seen to go in followed by a German nightfighter – both hit the ground. It was a night when everyone was tense and a bit stewed up.

Historical research is now clear in providing the evidence for the essential contribution of the heavy bombers in the run-up to D-Day, the beach assault itself, and the development of the Normandy campaign. A German Air Ministry report of 13 June stated that the raids had 'caused the breakdown of all main lines; the coastal defences have been cut off' and 'large-scale strategic movement of German troops by rail is practically impossible'.

Throughout the Normandy campaign Bomber Command had also been tasked with countering the V-1, the flying-bomb, offensive. This campaign is often overlooked, yet Bomber Command dropped a greater tonnage of bombs on V-weapon targets than on Berlin in the entire war. For some this counter-offensive was personal. Ron Winton flew as a wireless operator with No. 207 Squadron. 'My home was at Dagenham in Essex at the time, and as it was in the direct line with London it was being heavily attacked by the V-1. So

Right Oblique aerial photograph showing the entrances to the subterranean tunnels at Saint-Leu d'Esserent, northwest of Paris, which were used by the Germans to store flying bombs. An accurate attack by aircraft mainly of No. 5 Group on the night of 7/8 July 1944 succeeded in causing a landslide, which blocked the tunnel entrances. *Far right* RAF and WAAF intelligence officers and their staff at work in the Map Section in the Operations Block at Bomber Command HQ, High Wycombe, Buckinghamshire, in 1944. (Air Historical Branch)

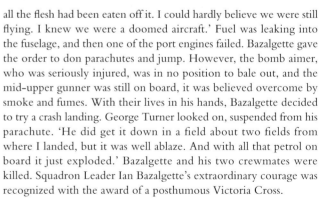

told his pilot that the fire was spreading: 'When it burns the spar the wing will go, and when the wing goes, we go.' Russell gave the order to bale out. From the crew of eight, all would survive except one man.

He picked up his parachute by the release handle instead of the proper handle and released the parachute in the aircraft. All we could do was tell him to clip it on and hang on as there was a little umbrella chute that acted as the pilot chute. We said hang on to that and when you get clear let it go and it should take the parachute. Obviously it didn't and unfortunately his body wasn't found until November.

In August 1944 one attack on a V-1 target resulted in an extraordinary act of bravery. On 4 August 1944 Ian Bazalgette's No. 635 Lancaster was struck by flak when it was attacking the flying-bomb depot at Trossy Saint-Maximin – the starboard wing engines were taken out and flames spread. George Turner, the flight engineer, recalled: 'The starboard wing was one mass of flames, with pieces flying off it. In fact it was more like a skeleton.' Doug Cameron, the rear gunner, recalled that the wing was 'like a herringbone after

all the flesh had been eaten off it. I could hardly believe we were still flying. I knew we were a doomed aircraft.' Fuel was leaking into the fuselage, and then one of the port engines failed. Bazalgette gave the order to don parachutes and jump. However, the bomb aimer, who was seriously injured, was in no position to bale out, and the mid-upper gunner was still on board, it was believed overcome by smoke and fumes. With their lives in his hands, Bazalgette decided to try a crash landing. George Turner looked on, suspended from his parachute. 'He did get it down in a field about two fields from where I landed, but it was well ablaze. And with all that petrol on board it just exploded.' Bazalgette and his two crewmates were killed. Squadron Leader Ian Bazalgette's extraordinary courage was recognized with the award of a posthumous Victoria Cross.

Into September 1944, and with scenes of liberation in their wake, the Allied armies edged towards Germany. Bomber Command was going to be returning to Germany in force, its strength greater in terms of aircrew and aircraft numbers than it had ever been before, its destructive potential vastly superior than at any stage during the previous five years.

'What a trip for a third.'

Mailly-le-Camp
3/4.5.1944

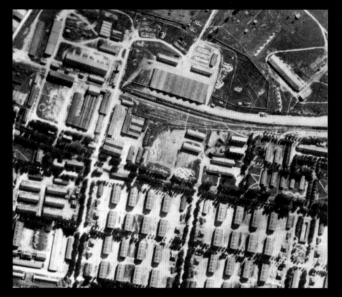

Left **Before and after reconnaissance photographs clearly display the success of the Bomber Command attack on Mailly-le-Camp.** (Air Historical Branch)

3 May 1944 is like any other day in Bomber Command's history. But by the end of it, it proves to be a disaster at least comparable to the losses taken over Leipzig in February and eclipsed only by Nuremberg a month previously. Indeed, percentage losses are greater. The only difference perhaps is that, whereas Nuremberg can be seen as the Royal Air Force's equivalent to the Charge of the Light Brigade, the attack on Mailly-le-Camp is, at least in terms of its objectives, a success. Both disasters, however, could have been avoided.

As at Nuremberg, no one briefed that day anticipates disaster. Many crews are indeed quite bullish by this stage of the war. The invasion can only be just around the corner, and the Germans are being beaten on all fronts. The main irritation is that a trip to northern France now counts as only a third of an op, because it is considered 'easy'.

Bomber airfields across the country are alive with activity. It is a pleasant morning, and the ground crews once again set about their task with meticulous diligence. It is the bomb load that has aroused the most interest and sparks the fiercest debate. Gone are the incendiaries in favour of more heavy explosive: a typical load of one 4,000lb Cookie and 16 x 500lb Medium Capacity bombs suggests a target where destructive power is more important than fire.

At briefing, the intelligence officers are similarly meticulous. London has been informed via the Resistance that the Germans have assembled a mass of armour and men at Mailly-le-Camp in the Champagne region of France. It is believed that the depot houses 21st Panzer Divisional HQ, three Panzer battalions, and possibly the remnants of two other battalions withdrawn from the Eastern Front. It also comprises motorized transport (MT) buildings and workshops, a tank training ground, firing range, and barrack accommodation for some 5,000 troops. The timing of the attack is to coincide with the troops' return to barracks at midnight to ensure maximum destruction. Unusually, briefing covers three aiming points.

The operation is a joint effort between two bomber groups. A 'special duties' squadron will also be interspersed within the stream to enable a consistent 'layer' of jamming, to confuse the German nightfighters. Aiming point marking is to be provided by Mosquitoes, with the whole attack controlled by a Master of Ceremonies.

For most of the crews, the early part of the raid passes without incident. The weather is clear, with good visibility, and the moon is bright. The bomber stream heads towards a pre-designated assembly point some fifteen miles north of their target and waits. They do not know it yet, but they are heading for a trap. Not a deliberate trap, where the Germans have any prior knowledge of the raid, but rather a trap resulting from delays in the target marking and a breakdown in communication between the markers, the Master of Ceremonies, and the Main Force.

As they circle, crews become restless. Aircraft begin exploding in the sky, the victims of nightfighters that have rushed to the area. Conditions are perfect for them. The cause is a liturgy of over-complicated planning, poor communication, and simple bad luck. The instructions from the Master of Ceremonies for the Main Force to come in and bomb have not been heard. Additional communication from the Deputy is drowned out by an American Forces radio broadcast and backchat from a handful of the Main Force crews who by now are convinced that the raid is going disastrously wrong. Ron

Eeles, a rear gunner, remembers hearing 'Deep in the heart of Texas' followed by applause and what sounds like a party: 'Other garbled talk was in the background but drowned by the music,' he says.

The effect is further delay and almost inevitably disaster. Confusion means precious minutes are wasted, allowing the German controllers to vector their aircraft to the Lancasters' assembly point and the flak gunners to find their range, with the resultant mayhem. Ted Manners, a special duties operator tasked with listening for and jamming the commands from the German nightfighter controllers, cannot work fast enough: 'I didn't have to tell the gunners that there were nightfighters about because they could see that for themselves,' he says.

Finally some semblance of control is established, and the bombs begin to fall, wreaking havoc below. Several enormous explosions can be seen – and felt – as more than one of the Lancasters is caught in the shockwaves that reverberate through the night sky. Returning crews agree that it appears as though the target has been completely obliterated. Subsequent reports will indeed confirm that fact, with hundreds of soldiers killed, and large quantities of tanks and motorized transport destroyed. Several crews report a new phenomenon – 'scarecrows' – in the target area. A 'scarecrow' is believed to be a special weapon the Germans have devised to look like an aircraft exploding in the bomber stream. Whether myth or reality, at the time everyone thinks it strange that, if the Germans can invent a device to explode with such accuracy, then why can't they do the same with their 'ordinary' flak? The force of a 'scarecrow' bursting below one Lancaster convinces the pilot that what he has actually experienced is another aircraft exploding, and it might easily be one of the four Lancasters missing from his squadron.

Indeed, in terms of losses, it has been a terrible night for Bomber Command. When the final sums are done, 330 Lancasters reached the target area, but 42 have been destroyed. Of the airmen who went down with the bombers, 29 managed to evade capture and 21 have been taken prisoner. Some 255 are dead.

Rusty Waughman, a young Lancaster pilot, returns to base safely, but having fended off a determined nightfighter attack. He notes in his diary simply: 'Ops Mailly-le-Camp . . . What a trip for a third!'

Veterans in Portrait

Igraine Hamilton

Women's Auxiliary Air Force

Administration

Prior to joining the Women's Auxiliary Air Force, Igraine volunteered to nurture badly burned airmen through their recuperation while under the watch of Archibald McIndoe at the Queen Victoria Hospital, East Grinstead. Igraine went on to serve as a WAAF, at RAF Stradishall, which was home to numerous RAF Bomber Command squadrons.

The time with Archie McIndoe was incredible. My parents knew Archie, and he asked if I would go to the burns unit. Ward 3 was for burns sufferers, mostly airmen, but there were others, like a girl who had been working in a sugar factory that received a direct hit and she was covered in sugar – horrendous.

It was very free and easy. They could smoke and somebody would sit by the bed and help flick the ash and talk to them. I went to every bed, every day and read or wrote letters, or cashed cheques, anything that was needed. I would take them in wheelchairs to the cinema and sometimes take them home for the day. One went on television after the war and I rang him and said, 'Do you remember me wheeling you back in at two o'clock in the morning, drunk.' 'Yes, I do!' he replied.

If Archie had carried out an operation on somebody's eyes, then they hadn't seen me but we had been talking. They liked me to be at the end of the bed when the bandages came off, to see what I looked like – not in a personal way – they could put a face to a voice.

I joined up before I had to. I had the 'V' on my arm for volunteer. We had some close family friends who had lost a son, killed in the air force. And then there was the time in the burns unit.

At Stradishall I was in Administration. We did what we were told to do. A lot of Polish airmen came in and we had to get down on our hands and knees and scrub the place.

Our billets were right alongside the airfield and I was offered a trip on a raid over Berlin. They were going to pull up by the huts and let me on and then drop me off afterwards – a serious offer. I did think about it seriously,

and then thought it wasn't fair on my parents, as I was an only child. Later I went up in the tower and waited. They came back. It was very tense in the tower – particularly if somebody knew someone who was out, which was pretty much all the time. The next day I was offered a trip again and I thought, 'shall I, shan't I'. I didn't go. They didn't come back.

I had a cigarette case and I got people to sign it. Then I started to find that people who had signed it didn't come back. I gave it away. I couldn't cope with this happening anymore.

" *I don't think a lot of people realize what the airmen went through. They just say, 'Oh the bombers went over and bombed Berlin.' That's just a sentence. They don't think of the cramped conditions and never knowing what's going to happen. Some were terribly injured. Some became prisoners of war.*

And so many didn't come through. Bomber Command did an incredible job and the memorial is somewhere people can take the young, in particular, and make them realize that, if the airmen hadn't done all this, we wouldn't be here. **"**

Veterans in Portrait

Eileen Richards

Women's Auxiliary Air Force

MT Driver

Eileen served as a WAAF at RAF Stradishall, as part of the Motor Transport section, driving staff cars, ambulances, tractors pulling bomb trolleys, and often driving aircrews to and from their bombers prior to, and after, a raid.

We had a licence to drive vehicles up to 3 tons. We did crew coaches, taking the crews out to the aircraft. I was an ambulance driver for some of the time, and sometimes we would be asked to drive a staff car with a high-ranking officer, sometimes the ration wagon, when you drove round to all the different Messes. We did a lot of crew coaches, which we all liked because we would chat to the fellas.

We used to get leave, but we were always glad to get back. I used to get bored after a while. We had ten days leave four times a year and I always wanted to go back after five days seeing the family and being home. We were really like a lot of kids, all very young, most of us teenagers.

There was a dark side of it. When you picked up crews and took them out, you never discussed where they were going. They were very good at hiding their feelings, and we all tried to take our cue from them. We didn't want to admit that this was life and death. I think they would not have shown anything, but it must have been there, the fear. I always found that if you picked them up after they had been over they were very quiet. They were very tired but so quiet. I look back now and I feel so ... I can cry now about things more than I did then.

❝ *I am very happy that the nation has finally recognized the sacrifice of all those brave young men.* **❞**

Veterans in Portrait
Geoffrey Whitehead

Royal Air Force
Ground Crew

It was after technical training that Geoffrey Whitehead's 'feelings about the RAF became stronger'. Geoffrey joined No. 102 Squadron early in January 1942 as an instrument 'basher' and shortly afterwards was posted to No. 1652 Heavy Conversion Unit, where aircrew familiarized themselves with the four-engine bombers. Over time Geoffrey's regard for his flying colleagues grew.

I looked on the aircrew as heroes. When it came to getting to know them, there wasn't time. They would come and go – disappear, because they had either been killed or become prisoners. I did regard them as above criticism because of the job they were doing. The whole thing was a miraculous solution to the problem of Adolf Hitler. When I joined the air force I couldn't see a way through to how we were ever going to beat them. Then along comes this damn big team of bright people and immediately you could see the end of the tunnel. You could see that, whatever happens today or tomorrow, we shall smash them. The fact remains that we did win.

While serving with No. 1652 Conversion Unit, Geoffrey penned a poem, 'In Memoriam – Jack Titshall'.

'Jack Titshall's turn,' said Sergeant Brown
'To take the air test, fetch him Geoff.'
But when I told him he must fly,
Jack Titshall turned as pale as death.

'What ails thee lad?' said Sergeant Brown.
'The ground test's fine, you'll be all right.'
'It breaks my dream, that's all,' said Jack.
'My mother called me in the night.'

'She said she'd see me soon, quite soon,
And not to fear she'd stretch her hand
To free me from the burning plane
And take me to the Promised Land.'

'Pilot to base, air test complete.'
'Then back you come,' the tower called.
But as he lowered flaps and wheels
The stresses rose, the aircraft stalled.

We watched the fire engines race
Towards that wall of fire and flame
And Sergeant Brown said, 'Steady lads.
Let's hope to God his mother came.'

❝ *It's high time we had the memorial. People forgot what we had all done, within months – of all the people who died to give them their freedom.* **❞**

Sidney 'Buzz' Spilman

Royal New Zealand Air Force

Pilot

In the first four months of 1945 Sidney 'Buzz' Spilman completed a full tour with No. 75 (NZ) Squadron. On his first operation, a daylight to Ludwigshafen on 5 January 1945, his crew was joined by their flight commander, with Buzz acting as second dickie – to gain experience. 'I remember that raid all right. They routed us along the same line as the city is built along the banks of the Rhine, so it was not a quick crossing of the defended area. We could see ahead and the aircraft in front were getting a hiding.'

In 1941 Buzz Spilman completed the first stage of his flying training in New Zealand and, following a crossing of the Pacific Ocean to Canada, he was entrained to continue his journey east. 'We got as far as Ottawa and heard that the Japanese had attacked Pearl Harbor. That came as a complete surprise and we thought we would be sent home to defend New Zealand. But they sent us on to Halifax and then across the Atlantic to Liverpool. When we arrived we could still see the rubble from the bombing.'

Buzz was destined to carry out two years as a flying instructor prior to a posting to an operational squadron, where he was able to utilize much of the flying

experience he had gained while instructing. On many occasions Buzz's flying abilities and situational awareness ensured his crew survived to fly and fight again. On one operation it became clear that the briefed wind speeds and directions were incorrect. 'It was quite a lot stronger.' By the time recalculations had been made, they were ten minutes late on target. 'We were isolated, at the end of the queue you might say. We started pushing Window out.' Buzz's rear gunner reported back how the German anti-aircraft were giving the Window 'the works', telling his crewmates to 'Keep it going! Keep it coming out!'

The Germans were firing at the Window. It disturbed their radar and they didn't know which was an aircraft and which was reflective metal foil. That saved us that night. It's a pretty scary feeling by yourself – the target all lit up and everybody else gone.

On another night raid Buzz recalls that it soon became clear that enemy nightfighters had picked up the main stream of bombers. Buzz, at the controls of his Lancaster, suddenly became aware of a fighter flare dropped from above.

It lit up the whole sky. That was pretty scary – illuminating all the aircraft. Only briefly, but they knew where we were and could go after us individually. I dropped a couple of thousand feet – stuck the aircraft into a dive to get out of the area. If there is any light in the sky, it's up. Looking down, it's dark, so you go down to the darkest part of the sky and try to evade. You don't try to set up a fight. The fighter has all the advantage.

On a further night raid, however, an enemy fighter did close within range.

We were approaching the target and the rear gunner spotted a single-engine aircraft flying at the same height just off to the

port side. He had his speed and height right and must have seen us – he was close enough for us to see him. I said to the rear gunner 'Hold him in your sights.' I also called to the mid-upper gunner to train his guns on him. I said, 'When I hear the guns going off I am going to corkscrew.' They went off and I dived down – there wasn't any point in staying! The fighter was off too, diving, but whether we hit him I don't know. I talked to the gunners who thought they did see our bullets bouncing off the aircraft.

Buzz applied the tactic of never flying straight and level – always making slight alterations. On one night Buzz was 'flying along minding my own business. The sky was clear and quiet although there was the occasional bump from the slipstream of an aircraft.'

Suddenly the sky was lit up in front. A flash, and a bomber was illuminated – the flash just above its left wing. Then an explosion just under the right wing and a third right behind the tail. They nearly got him but he was still flying. It was one of ours and when we got back I had a look at it. The wing on the left had a neat round hole where the shell went right through before it exploded. The one on the right made the wing look like a pepper pot and it's a wonder it stayed together. From the third explosion there was not a scratch. I thought the rear gunner would have been killed – the explosion was right under his seat but the angle must have taken the shrapnel in the same direction as the gun, some distance away, was pointing. The shrapnel missed. They nearly got that aircraft but it got back – only just.

But on another occasion another crew were not so fortunate.

There was a complete explosion in front. I never saw any of the aircraft parts. You naturally duck your head – I thought the undercarriage or something would be coming back on to us – we were right behind it. But the bomber just disappeared. The guys didn't have a chance. They must have hit the bombs.

On 28 June 2012 Buzz Spilman, within a party of New Zealand Bomber Command veterans, attended the dedication and unveiling of the Bomber Command Memorial.

" *It's a long time since all these events happened. Families have been grieving for their lost ones and there's never been a resolution. A lot of blokes that were lost haven't even got a burial spot. It's wonderful that they can now be acknowledged. We have had a full life. We are the lucky ones that came out of it. The guys that didn't make it were caught up in it the same as we were, but their fate was decided for them at a time when they were just reaching the peak of their manhood – their whole life in front of them, lost to them. The price of war.* **"**

Bomber Command at War

September 1944–May 1945

Following the liberation of France and the advance towards Germany, Bomber Command's attention shifted back towards carrying the war directly to the Third Reich. The bomber war was once more being waged over Germany, and once more the crews battled their way through the aerial and ground defences. On 10 September 1944, on a raid to Frankfurt, Australian Bill Pearce could do little when his aircraft came under attack.

We were attacked by nightfighters four times. Thanks to the gunner's alertness and the skipper's skills, we fought our way out. I hung on in the cabin, my stomach in a very tight knot, listening to it on the intercom, and expecting something to happen at any moment. After each engagement, the skipper would settle us down with a few quiet words.

What happens during a nightfighter attack is a violent evasive action manoeuvre called the 'corkscrew'. This is carried out by the pilot, on instructions from the gunners, firstly diving in the direction of the attack, and then continually changing direction while diving and climbing, to give the effect of a corkscrew track through the air. The idea is to alter the angle at which the fighter must aim to try and hit the bomber, a continual alteration of the deflection angle.

I was hanging on in the cabin. At the bottom of a dive my stomach would be forced down towards my boots, and at the top of the climb and then the start of a dive, I would float up off my seat. I would be held there by jamming my knees under my small desk. My parachute pack would float up off the floor and then settle back again at the bottom of the dive.

I would hear our guns being fired. This came over the intercom as

a 'tick tick tick' noise, and I could smell the burning cordite from the gasses caused by the exploding ammunition. All the while I would wait for something to happen to our aircraft, like the awful explosive noise as bullets or cannon shells find a mark. To 'get away with it' was a good feeling, but not really felt until I climbed out of the aircraft at our dispersal area, and once again had my feet on the ground.

Three main targeting systems were now emphasized: attacking synthetic oil, destroying and dislocating enemy transport systems, and maintaining the attacks on German industrial centres. Debate continued at command level as to where best to focus the bombing. Ultimately all three systems would be attacked, and the aircrews would find themselves carrying out quite diverse operational duties, perhaps supporting the land campaigns in daylight one day and then performing a deep night penetration on their following operation. On New Year's Day 1945, 102 Lancasters and 2 Mosquitoes breached the Dortmund–Ems canal, a transportation target, a raid on which No. 9 Squadron's George Thompson was awarded a posthumous Victoria Cross – having died from burns suffered while rescuing his two air gunners from their burning turrets. On the same day 17 Mosquitoes attacked rail tunnels through which German reinforcements and supplies could pass to the 'Battle of the Bulge' raging in the Ardennes. Then, that night, 598 aircraft were involved in numerous raids, the main effort being against the Mitteland canal, the railyards at Vohwinkel, and the benzol works at Dortmund.

In the final months of the war there were some extraordinary highlights demonstrating the efficacy of the bombing at this stage

Right **Ground crew on a Bomber Command station return the V-sign to a neighbouring searchlight as they celebrate VE Day, 8 May 1945.** (Air Historical Branch)

of the war and the significant developments that had taken place in the abilities of the Command – all within an extraordinarily diverse context, spanning precision bombing, area bombing or humanitarian missions.

No clearer example of precision bombing can be found than the successful attack on the German battleship *Tirpitz* by Lancasters of Nos 9 and 617 Squadrons on 12 November 1944. Direct hits by 12,000lb Tallboys capsized the 'beast' as she skulked in a Norwegian fjord. The Secretary of State for Air conveyed his congratulations to the crews. 'The destruction of the *Tirpitz* must rank with the finest feats of Bomber Command and marks a further stage in the crumbling of German power.'

No greater example of the incredible destructive potential of Bomber Command can be found than the attack carried out on the night of 14/15 February 1945 – the firestorming of Dresden. Encouraged by Winston Churchill, the Air Ministry tasked Bomber Command with attacking communications centres behind German lines on the Eastern Front. The devastation was unprecedented, and tens of thousands of lives were lost on the ground. Disgracefully, Churchill attempted to distance himself from the attack shortly after the raid – the first of many snubs to Bomber Command, culminating in, among other acts, the omission of a mention for the Command in Churchill's post-war victory speech and the denial of a specific campaign medal.

No finer examples of humanitarian missions can be found than Operation 'Exodus', the transporting of POWs back to the UK, and Operation 'Manna', the dropping of around 6,672 tons of desperately needed food to the starving population of western Holland. Tony Farrell served as a Mosquito pilot with No. 105 Squadron. 'One final episode that was most impressive concerned the mercy missions, a brief campaign to feed the starving Dutch with air drops of food. From 2 May 1945 up to VE Day on 8 May I did four of these, marking dropping zones for the heavies on airfields and racecourses. On 8 May, the last, we came down to ground level, and it was such a moving scene watching the hungry but jubilant Dutch swarming into the dropping zone and waving like mad.'

Right up to the end of the war, Bomber Command aircrews remained at the forefront of overall tactical and strategic develop-

ments. These volunteers continued to put their lives on the line – and many of these lives would be taken, including those of some of Bill Pearce's crewmates. Bill, in a No. 156 Squadron Lancaster, piloted by Desmond Pelly, was over Germany on the night of 20/21 February 1945. They had just started the bombing run when

what all Bomber Command aircrews feared might happen, did happen – to us. There was a loud, rendering, explosive 'whoomph'. It came from not very far from me, and I knew instantly what it was. We had been hit by either flak or gunfire from a nightfighter. I was later to find out we had been hit by a burst of 20mm cannon shell. It hit the tail and rear turret, killing my rear gunner, and then went into the starboard inner engine, elevators and petrol tanks. The engine immediately exploded and caught fire.

I remember I went cold all over. I felt this sensation surge through my body. My world was shattered to pieces around me, the pit of my stomach felt as though it had dropped down into my boots.

The Skipper came up on the intercom and ordered us to bale out. I immediately acknowledged this order with 'Wop bailing out.' I didn't have to be told twice.

Bill discarded his flying helmet and oxygen mask, and as he climbed his way through the fuselage to the rear door of the Lancaster he started to feel the effect of the lack of oxygen. 'I was feeling very light-headed and I remember thinking I had better get moving.'

Below Target indicators, flak and a photo-flash light up the night sky over Pforzheim during a devastating Bomber Command raid in February 1945. *Right* Aircrew veterans will always comment on the crucial roles of their non-flying colleagues. Here ground crew warm themselves on a stove in the snow at RAF Rufforth, Yorkshire, before venturing on to the dispersal behind them to service a Handley Page Halifax of No. 1663 Heavy Conversion Unit. (Air Historical Branch)

Opposite page and right **Ground crew loading food supplies as part of Operation 'Manna'. Between 29 April and 7 May 1945, Bomber Command aircrews dropped 6,672 tons of food to the starving populace of a large area in western Holland still in German hands.** (Air Historical Branch)

My mid-upper gunner was there before me. He had opened the door and was standing in the doorway. I was just able to tap him on the shoulder as he went out. However, he had made a fatal mistake – he had picked up the parachute pack by the shiny handle, the 'D' handle of the ripcord, and the pilot chute had exploded in the aircraft. He had clipped the 'chute to his harness and gathered the canopy in his arms. I remember seeing the folds of white silk as he stood in the doorway. His body was found later on the ground, still attached to his parachute and harness. I think his death was caused when he left the aircraft. Even in my light-headed lack-of-oxygen condition, I saw his body go below the tailplane and the open 'chute canopy go over the top of it. He was then pulled back to, and around and over, the tailplane and was probably killed by the impact.

I was crouched over the doorsill. I remember looking at the fire in the wing, around the engine nacelle and thinking 'Gee, that sure is burning well.' I must have leaned a bit further out, I was torn out of the aircraft by the slipstream, and fell head over heels through space. After tumbling for what seemed an age, I thought, 'Well I'd better pull it now.' I found the ripcord handle and pulled it. The 'chute opened, my descent was halted, and I was left suspended, in the middle of a black void.

As I hung there, with the dark night around me, I was overcome by a feeling of absolute loneliness. The cold and the lower altitude brought me

back to my proper senses, but then I could hear other aircraft 'swishing' past me. They must have been above me, but I had the frightening thought of what would happen if one of them hit me. These aircraft soon passed on, and I was left hanging there in complete silence, in the darkness, and absolute loneliness.

Bill eventually came to earth – 'crashed in an ungainly heap'. Over the next few days he attempted to make his way out of Germany to friendlier territory, but his luck eventually ran out. He was captured on the outskirts of Cologne and saw out the war as a POW – one of 9,838 Bomber Command airmen who had become prisoners.

The first week of May 1945 saw the ultimate and total defeat of Nazi Germany and the unconditional surrender to the Allies. Thus concluded over five and a half years of war, throughout which the men of Bomber Command had been fighting continually. Of the 125,000 volunteer aircrew, 55,573 were either buried in the UK or on the European mainland, or had simply not been found – perhaps lost at sea, perhaps incinerated in a burning aircraft, or perhaps still in their aircraft and yet to be found.

Without any official recognition of the Bomber Boys' service, relatives of Bomber Command airmen, close friends, village and town councils, museums, veterans' associations, enthusiasts, historians and authors, from across the world, played their part in commemorating the 'Many' who had sacrificed all with small memorials and tributes: the striking No. 158 Squadron memorial at Lissett in the UK; Canada's Bomber Command Memorial at Nanton, Alberta; the memorial at Swartkop, which includes recognition of those killed while training as part of the British Commonwealth Air Training Plan in South Africa. And then, of course, there are the legions of Commonwealth War Graves Commission headstones marking the place of burial of individual airmen – or perhaps the collective grave of crewmates.

But now there is a place for international focus and commemoration. It has taken sixty-seven years, but a dedicated group of volunteers has galvanized public interest and financial support and has provided a place where the nations who defeated Nazism, and who remain free, can recognize 55,573 of those who fought the Second World War air battle and died for our freedom.

'What have they done to my Squadron?'

Cologne/Gremberg
23.12.1944

The Ardennes. 16 December 1944. German Panzers spearhead a surprise attack that smashes through thinly held Allied lines, catching the US commanders completely off guard. For many weeks, the Germans have been stockpiling tanks and guns for a bold strike that aims to slice the Allied armies in two and recapture the port of Antwerp. They have thrown everything into one last gamble, but it is a gamble that relies on the supply of men, munitions, and above all fuel continuing to reach the front line, to exploit the 'bulge' that has already been created and that would later lend its name to the battle.

The Germans have not only the element of surprise but also the weather on their side. Time and again, Pathfinder bomber crews at two airfields in England, Little Staughton and Graveley, are briefed to attack the railway marshalling yards in the Gremberg district of Cologne – yards that are critical to the German supply route – only to have their attack postponed. At the third time of asking, and despite atrocious weather, the decision is finally made to go.

Many of those taking part are experienced Bomber Boys, with at least forty or fifty operations behind them. But even they are nervous. Gerry Bennington DFM, a flight engineer, is left to ponder – after so many delays, how could the Germans not know they were coming: 'There was no way a secret like that could have been kept,' he says.

The attack involves only a small number of aircraft in three formations, with each formation led by a Lancaster equipped with a blind bombing device known as 'Oboe', accompanied by an Oboe-equipped Mosquito in reserve. 'Oboe' enables the bombers to attack even when the target is completely obscured by cloud. In a 'Heavy Oboe' attack, when the device is installed in a heavy bomber, the equipment comes with an additional 'crew' – the regular Lancaster crew is supplemented by a specialist Oboe pilot and navigator, who literally swap seats with their hosts for the bombing run.

Oboe has few vices, as long as the bombers remain hidden. The principal drawback is that it requires the pilot to fly straight and level for ten minutes in order to maintain the necessary 'signal' for when to release the bombs, and on whose lead the rest of the formation will also attack in salvo. It is also prone to technical problems, hence the need for a reserve Mosquito ready to take over in case of failure.

After a take-off in thick fog, the operation gets off to a dreadful start when two aircraft lose sight of one another in the cloud and

Right **Squadron Leader Robert Palmer VC, DFC and Bar.** (Air Historical Branch)

DFM, to remark: 'The Germans had plenty of practice by the time we arrived!' The navigator in one of the reserve Mosquitoes, Gordon Musgrove DFC, is similarly matter of fact: 'Such an opportunity [for the gunners] comes only once in a lifetime and I doubt if they ever worked so feverishly to fire as many shells in the shortest space of time.'

And then, just when they think things cannot get any worse, they do. A squadron of German fighters appears on the scene. It is a slaughter. Despite his aircraft being hit and catching fire, Palmer, courageously, flies on, believing that, if he breaks formation, the whole attack will have to be abandoned. As the signal for release comes, he drops his bombs, and almost immediately the aircraft falls into a spin, out of control. Palmer pays for such courage with his life, and receives the Victoria Cross for displaying 'heroic endeavour beyond praise'. The reserve Oboe Mosquito is also hit, and plunges burning to the ground.

The fight for survival begins, as the aircraft that have avoided the flak now come under sustained fighter attack. Four more Lancasters are plucked from the air, and the gin sky is suddenly full of tracer fire, burning aircraft, and the odd white speck and brown smudge of an open parachute and its owner. One pilot – Captain Edwin Swales, another future VC – fights a running battle lasting fifteen minutes before reaching safety. On all of the returning aircraft there are the scars of battle: dented fuselages, battered cockpits, shattered men.

The shock among those who have taken part is palpable. From one squadron alone twenty-seven men have been killed or at that moment are unaccounted for. While some will later return, for others it has been their final journey. The commanding officer at Graveley, Group Captain 'Dixie' Dean, is distraught: 'What have they done to my Squadron?'

Eight aircraft out of an attacking force of thirty fail to return – more than a quarter of the force destroyed at a time when Bomber Command has given up reporting losses in percentages because the numbers have become so small as to lose their meaning. More than fifty men are 'missing', though some will later turn up safe as prisoners of war.

The raid succeeds in causing considerable damage; five days later, Bomber Command returns to finish the job.

collide, killing all on board. It is an ominous sign. And it gets worse. Rather than the thick cloud they have been promised over the target, the three formations arrive to find a brilliant clear blue sky. Someone has blundered.

Despite the change in conditions, there is confusion among the crews as to whether to break formation and bomb individually, or carry on and bomb on their leader, as they have been briefed. Squadron Leader Robert Palmer, the Oboe pilot in the lead aircraft, takes his seat for the Oboe run. His navigator listens to the Oboe signal for the release point.

Heavy, predicted flak is being thrown their way. The German defences are having a field day. Watching the aircraft flying straight and level at a constant height and speed, they have ten minutes to loose off as many shells as they can. It is ten minutes of target practice where they simply cannot miss. And they don't. All of the first formation is hit, prompting one flight engineer, Tom Williamson

Veterans in Portrait
Dave Fellowes

Royal Air Force

Air Gunner

Dave served in the rear turret of a Lancaster bomber with No. 460 Squadron and then went on to No. 206 Squadron. Dave is credited with thirty-three bombing operations and survived a mid-air collision with another Lancaster, whose crew were not so fortunate, on the night of 7/8 January 1945.

We had expected bad weather and we were in cloud, coming up towards Munster. It was bumpy. It was horrible. We had a quick crew conference – should we climb and get out of this? It was not very nice. The answer was yes and the skipper called to the engineer for climbing power, and we started to climb. Being the rear gunner, I couldn't see anything in the cloud. Then all of a sudden it was bright. I could see other aeroplanes that had been up there a long time before us. Just as we were coming out of the cloud somebody said, 'Christ. We're hit!' and there was a crash, a rendering and tearing of metal, and a thump. Some other aircraft had come out of the cloud just below us and stuck his port wing into us, right under the mid-upper turret. Somebody saw the other aircraft just flick over and

after a short while we heard the bombs on board go off after it had hit the ground. We went into a spin and the skipper, after about 3,000 feet, got it out. He said, 'I'm going to try and open the bomb doors, if there's any hydraulics.' We did open the bomb doors and dropped our bombs. Then it was a case of sorting the aircraft out, turn around, and try and get home. We started to slow climb to get above the icing level to start with. The mid-upper gunner was helped out of his turret – there was no floor underneath him. That part of the aircraft had disappeared, from the bomb bay right back to the main door. The starboard aileron was all buckled, and over 3 feet of wing tip on the starboard side had gone. I was left up the back and my skipper said, 'David, if you want to, and I wouldn't blame

you, you can bale out.' We knew it was now friendly down below. I said, 'What? No! You could still get jumped by a fighter out here. If you are staying up here, I'm staying up here.'

While we were up at altitude, the skipper said, 'I'm going to try and lower the flaps to see if they come down, and the undercarriage.' We didn't want to do a belly landing, and fortunately the wheels did come down. We landed at Manston and a pick-up truck came round and showed us to the place where they dumped aeroplanes. We got out and when we saw the amount of damage we just couldn't believe it. We all reckoned we owed our lives to Avros – they built a good aeroplane.

A couple of nights later we were out again – to Stuttgart. I had noticed two Halifaxes down on our port side and a Lancaster on our starboard side, up a bit. We were going through, and around the back of the two Halifaxes came a Ju88. Prior to that the wireless operator had said he had seen a FW190 go over the top of us, most likely working with this Ju88. I opened fire and he opened fire at the same time. I can still see cannon tracer whizzing past me either side, and not one touched me. Our mid-upper, he got either a piece of shrapnel or a bullet in the neck. He survived but had to be taken and put on the rest bunk and given morphine. I was firing at the fighter and it came into 150 yards. We were both pumping lead at each other. I didn't have time to be scared. I've got to fight him – he's fighting me. The next thing I saw he tipped over on one wing and went straight down into a dive. Later we put in a claim and it was eventually credited to us. Our aircraft received damage in the fuel tanks – a couple of incendiary bullets. Thank God they hadn't gone off. There were quite a few holes. We came back home, had a glass of rum, had debriefing. You didn't think about it an awful lot – didn't have time to think about it. I reckon if you had dwelt upon it you wouldn't have done it again. My job was the next trip.

66 *From the end of the war and many years after, Sir Arthur Harris and us 'Old Lags', as he affectionately called his aircrew, suffered much verbal abuse from those in 'high*

places' for the damage done to Germany. Perhaps they could not remember the morale boost given to the British people when they heard on the radio that Bomber Command had attacked another German city, often at great cost to crews and aircraft. No – we were best forgotten.

It has taken some sixty-seven years for the 'Bomber Boys' to have this memorial to their lost comrades, and I for one am honoured to have helped in it coming to fruition. **99**

Arthur Smith

Royal Air Force

Flight Engineer

$\mathbf{B}$orn in 1925, Arthur Smith grew up in the Croydon area, south London. His interest in aviation was sparked by the activities at the nearby Croydon airport, and his father had become involved at Hendon.

When the war started I took a dislike to Germany obviously, and I was determined to get in the RAF. I volunteered at 16 ¹/₂. When I got in I thought about pilot, navigator, bomb aimer training but that meant I would be out in Canada, America or South Africa for a couple of years of training and I thought I would miss the war – young and foolhardy I suppose.

Prior to joining the RAF, Arthur had experienced the war at first hand in London. 'German fighters used to come over and strafe the park at the end of the road. What with the Blitz there was a real determination to get involved in the war.'

In November 1944 Arthur arrived at No. 50 Squadron to carry out his flight engineer duties as part of an Avro Lancaster crew.

Once you had a crew you had a family. You met other crews but you didn't get too involved. We were in a hut with beds down one side and also down the other. One crew one side. Another crew the other side. If you got too friendly with them then when you woke up in the morning and found their beds had not been slept in, that hurt. You tried to put yourself in a little cocoon with your crew.

A month before the end of the war Arthur's crew received instructions to prepare for a mid-afternoon take-off. They would be operating as part of a small force detailed to attack the U-boat and oil storage facilities at Hamburg.

We were escorting No. 617 Squadron. It was daylight and No. 617 Squadron were carrying their big, heavy bombs. They had reduced armament because of the weight. So we were given the orders to fly around the outside and give them protection. It was a sunny afternoon and I suddenly saw these enemy aircraft appear. I had never seen anything like it before in my life. There were no props on these aircraft. We found out afterwards that they were Me262s. I saw some of our aircraft go down on fire. To see that – horrible – the trauma.

As the war in Europe drew to a close, Arthur found himself taking part in Operation 'Exodus' – the return of Allied prisoners of war to the UK.

On VE Day we were flying back POWs from Brussels to Blackbushe – five or six trips a day. You could only bring about twelve, because there was nowhere specific for them in the Lancaster. They just sat anywhere they could. As soon as we landed at Blackbushe, a WAAF and a nurse would come to the aircraft. They would greet the first one and take hold of his arms and they would be taken for a bath and a meal. It was wonderful. After all the trauma they had been through and now to be grabbed hold of by two lovely young ladies. That happened to each one as they got off. We would turn around and go off to pick up another load.

66 *Most people, in any other service, have all been recognized. We were not recognized – disinherited really. That hurt inwardly, because we thought we had done a good job. I would have liked to have taken certain people on an operation with us to show them what it was like. We were forgotten. I never thought the memorial would come to fruition.* 99

Dedication and Unveiling

James Linehan

James's No. 57 Squadron Vickers Wellington was lost without trace on a raid to Hamburg on the night of 8/9 April 1942. The names of the entire crew are etched on the walls of the Runnymede Memorial.

In a month that would become the wettest June on record, the rain clouds disappeared for one day only – 28 June, the day of the memorial's unveiling.

As veterans and relatives of airmen who died in the war gathered in the glorious sunshine that bathed Green Park, many of them mused on whether 55,573 souls had called in a favour from someone up above.

With a 1,000-seat stand erected in front of the memorial, the scene was set for the arrival of Her Majesty The Queen, who was to perform the unveiling, and no fewer than eleven other members of the royal family who had asked to attend. Among the 6,500 widows, children and comrades of those who had died serving with Bomber Command were more than 250 who had flown from Australia, 39 from New Zealand, 42 from Canada, and others from Allied nations including Norway, the Czech Republic, the USA and Russia.

But one person who was missing was Robin Gibb, the man whose determination to see a memorial built got the project off the ground five years earlier. Tragically, Robin died on 20 May, just five weeks before the unveiling, after a long battle with cancer. As he lay in hospital, he had asked his wife, Dwina, and son, RJ, to keep him updated on the progress of the memorial, determined to make it to the ceremony. Dwina, who attended the unveiling (and donated the royalties from Robin's song 'Don't Cry Alone', to the memorial appeal), said: 'We're so proud. It's a tragedy that Robin couldn't be here. He was really looking forward to it, and it was one of his goals. But it's a wonderful achievement.'

The ceremony began with the thirteen Squadron Standards of the remaining Second World War bomber squadrons, followed by the arrival of the Duke of York, the Earl and Countess of Wessex, the Duke and Duchess of Gloucester, the Duke of Kent and Prince and Princess Michael of Kent. The Prince of Wales, newly promoted to Marshal of the Royal Air Force, and the Duchess of Cornwall arrived in their Rolls-Royce, and, following a fanfare by trumpeters of the Central Band of the Royal Air Force, the Queen and the Duke of Edinburgh arrived in a Bentley and took their places, after being introduced to major donors Lord Ashcroft, John Caudwell and Richard Desmond.

Following the singing of the National Anthem, Malcolm White, Chairman of the Bomber Command Association, made the welcome address. 'This is a profound moment, a moment which has been a long time coming,' he said. 'This place, and the memorial, will be an enduring feature on London's landscape, and I suggest it will be much more than that; a place to remind and reflect, and a haven to remember the men of Bomber Command.' He invited the Queen to unveil Philip Jackson's sculpture, and, after a hefty tug on a length of rope, the blue silk covers parted and the seven airmen were revealed to loud and approving applause.

In the blistering heat, the first victim of sunstroke lasted long enough to see the sculpture unveiled before being carried to a first-aid tent by St John Ambulance volunteers. Several other veterans would follow before the day was out.

The Venerable Ray Pentland, Chaplain-in-Chief of the Royal Air Force, then led a service of dedication and remembrance, giving

Page 112 **The dedication and unveiling of the Bomber Command Memorial** (via the RAFBF). *Opposite page* **Queen Elizabeth II, the Duke of Edinburgh, the Prince of Wales and Camilla, the Duchess of Cornwall attend the unveiling of the Bomber Command Memorial. Air Commodore Malcolm White, Chairman of the BCA, far left.** (Press Association) *This page, clockwise from top* **Sophie, Countess of Wessex, greets veterans** (via the RAFBF); **A salute to Bomber Command** (via the RAFBF); **Prince Charles chats to a veteran** (via the RAFBF); **The unveiling of the aircrew statue** (Press Association); **Richard Desmond (left) and Jim Dooley at the dedication and unveiling ceremony** (Tim Clarke via the *Daily Express*)

Page 116-117 (Tim Clarke via the *Daily Express*) ***This page, clockwise from top left*** **A Metropolitan police officer collects poppies dropped by the Battle of Britain Memorial Flight Lancaster to give to Bomber Command veterans** (Press Association); **Camilla, the Duchess of Cornwall talks to Bomber Command veteran New Zealander Dick Lempriere** (Press Association); **A Metropolitan police officer helps a Bomber Command veteran** (Fighting High); **Comrades down the ages. A veteran receives assistance from a modern RAF colleague** (Fighting High); **'Thank you sir.'** (Fighting High) ***Opposite page*** **The aircrew statue unveiled.** (Paul Grover)

thanks for 'those who laid down their lives in the cause of justice, freedom and peace'. He added 'By the costly and sacrificial endeavour of their service, the powers of evil and darkness were defeated and overcome.' In a formal dedication of the memorial, he said: 'May it remind us, and all who pass by, of the freedom and liberty that was bought for us through the bravery and skill of the aircrew; and of the commitment of all those who supported them on the ground.'

In a service that included the hymns 'Praise my Soul, the King of Heaven' and 'O God, Our Help in Ages Past', Air Marshal Sir Robert Wright, Controller of the RAF Benevolent Fund, read from Isiah 40: 28–31, saying: 'Those who hope in the Lord will renew their strength. They will soar on wings like eagles, they will run and not grow weary, they will walk and not be faint.'

Air Chief Marshal Sir Stephen Dalton, Chief of the Air Staff, also gave an address, recounting the story of Canadian Pilot Officer Andrew Mynarski, who was awarded the Victoria Cross posthumously for trying to help his rear gunner out of a burning Lancaster, and forfeiting his own life in the process. He also spoke of one of the veterans at the ceremony, 99-year-old Wing Commander James Flint, awarded the George Medal for going back into his ditched and sinking bomber in the North Sea to save the life of his navigator. And he spoke of Operation 'Manna', when Bomber Command dropped almost 7,000 tons of food to the starving Dutch people in 1945 as they were being liberated. 'For their bravery and sacrifice, which helped to give us our freedom, we will never forget them,' he said.

The engines of five Tornado GR4 bombers roared their agreement as they flew in a tight V formation overhead, before the arrival of the one piece of machinery that can upstage even the Queen. Britain's last remaining airworthy Lancaster bomber, its Merlin engines vibrating the ribcages of all those on the ground below, flew over the memorial and scattered Green Park with poppies in a fitting salute to the fallen. When the Lancaster, part of the RAF's Battle of Britain Memorial Flight, took off from RAF Coningsby in Lincolnshire earlier that morning, the pilot requested clearance from the control tower by saying: 'This is Lancaster PA474 requesting permission for take-off. We have seven crew on board and 55,573 souls.' The bomb doors had been opened to drop the poppies by former No. 100 Squadron pilot Ron Clarke, who flew

Left **A meeting of veterans.** (via the Royal Air Force Benevolent Fund)

Right **Jessie Bowler, widow of Sergeant Ernest Thirkettle, a mid-upper gunner in a Lancaster that was shot down over Denmark on 4 September 1943. All the crew were killed. Ernest's body remains in the fuselage, which is buried deep in marshland. The crash site is his grave. Jessie is holding a picture of them both on their wedding day in November 1942.** (via the Royal Air Force Benevolent Fund)

Lancaster EE139 'Phantom of the Ruhr', in whose colours the port side of the BBMF's Lancaster is currently painted. On the ground, tears flowed freely among those who had lost husbands, fathers and friends a lifetime ago, most of whom never thought this day would come.

Then the honour of leading the congregation in the traditional words of remembrance fell to Douglas Radcliffe, whose chance comment five years earlier had lit the touchpaper for the memorial appeal. 'They shall grow not old as we that are left grow old: age shall not weary them, nor the years condemn. At the going down of the sun and in the morning, we will remember them.'

The service ended with a blessing and the veterans mingled with the Queen and other members of the royal family in the central section of the memorial to inspect approvingly the monument to so many heroes.

The event was screened by the BBC and Sky News, as well as being shown on giant screens in the 'Salute Area' in the south end of Green Park, where the 5,500 relatives and veterans who could not be accommodated in the tight space around the memorial watched the proceedings. Carol Vorderman, a patron of the Bomber Command Association, played host to all those in the 'Salute Area', where singers including the classical male vocal group Blake, Tori White and Jane McDonald kept the crowd entertained before and after the ceremony, giving their time for free. The RAF, meanwhile, provided hundreds of cadets to act as stewards and to keep the attendees cool with much-needed bottles of water and ice.

'Today is something which has been so long overdue,' said 90-year-old Peggy Mann, who was widowed in 1945 and has never remarried. 'It's been a perfectly tearful day because I'm so pleased they have got recognition at last.' Her daughter Wendy Price, 67, was born almost exactly nine months after Cyril Mann, 22, died when his Lancaster crash-landed on its return from his fourth operation. 'It is a gap in my life, never having known my father,' she said. 'It means a lot to me that this memorial has finally been built.'

'It does the boys proud,' said George 'Johnny' Johnson, one of only three remaining survivors of the Dam Busters raid. 'Worth waiting for.'

It may have taken sixty-seven years for the nation to show its

than expectation, and looking with a sense of disbelief at the end result, Jim Dooley said:

'One thing that always kept coming back to me as we tried to make this happen was a conversation I had with an elderly Dutchman when I visited the Netherlands to raise money there on the anniversary of Operation 'Manna'. I asked him why so many people turned out to applaud the Bomber Command veterans who were with me, and he said: 'You never know the true value of your freedom until someone takes it and keeps it from you with violence.' That, to me, summed up the reason it was so important to make sure future generations had something permanent to draw their attention to Bomber Command's pivotal contribution to the freedom we still enjoy today, and the collective sacrifice willingly made by so many men to achieve it.'

As anyone who has attempted anything on the sort of scale of the memorial knows, success is achieved not by one person, but by the commitment and dedication of hundreds of people, each of whom is a vital link in the chain that drags an idea from the drawing board into reality. At times the memorial faced serious roadblocks, and the members of the Memorial Committee felt as though they were being treated as nothing more than property developers as they grappled with the most appalling red tape and bureaucracy. But every time a daunting obstacle presented itself, someone with the necessary expertise stepped forward to help the veterans surmount it. As time went on, the veterans and fundraisers became convinced that the memorial was simply meant to be.

Sir William Blackburne's legal expertise was invaluable, as was the accounting know-how of John Boyes, the treasurer of the scheme.

When the campaign needed to win the support of the wider public, it found friends in the media who turned it into a national cause. Gordon Rayner of the *Daily Telegraph*, John Ingham of the *Daily Express*, Marco Giannangeli of the *Sunday Express*, David Willetts of the *Sun* and Robert Hardman of the *Daily Mail* all proved to be trusty allies, as did their newspapers.

The BBC, ITN and Sky brought the campaign to an even wider audience by televising the unveiling and broadcasting documentaries by John Sergeant and Alex Beetham, son of Sir Michael,

gratitude, but such was the scale of Bomber Command's losses that, if each of the 55,573 dead had been given their own day of remembrance since VE Day, it would take until 2 July 2097 to complete the roll-call.

John Bell, 89, who flew fifty operations as a bomb aimer with No. 617 Squadron, said: 'It's the end of a chapter. Over the years we thought it was never going to happen, but we have been amazed by the response of the public after the appeal to raise money for it began.'

Alan Finch, a Royal Australian Air Force pilot with No. 467 Squadron, was among those who had flown from the other side of the world, in his case from New South Wales, to take part in the ceremony. 'Only time I've ever come back to London,' he said. His take on the memorial? 'Bloody marvellous.'

As soon as the formalities were over, the public showed just how much the memorial meant to them by visiting in their thousands and leaving a steady stream of flowers, poppies and personal messages. Some left photocopies of letters sent to them by the Air Ministry and commanding officers informing them of the loss of a loved one; others hung from the statues pictures of their relatives, standing proudly by the aircraft in which they would lose their lives. Reflecting on the five-year campaign that had begun more in hope

Ian Bazalgette

Ian, who already held the Distinguished Flying Cross, was posthumously awarded a Victoria Cross. Ian, flying a No. 635 Squadron Avro Lancaster, died trying to save the lives of fellow crew members during a 4 August 1944 attack on the V-weapon site at Trossy Saint-Maximin. Ian is buried in Senantes Churchyard, France.

exploring the betrayal of Bomber Command after the war.

Douglas Radcliffe and Sebastian Cox waved the flag for the historical authenticity of the memorial and the vital input from veterans. Overseeing everyone were the steady hands and comforting reassurance of the Bomber Command Association President, Sir Michael Beetham, and successive chairmen Tony Iveson, Charles Clarke and Malcolm White.

Sixty-seven years were a long time to wait, and questions as to why Bomber Command was treated so badly by successive governments are likely to be debated for generations to come. But the sad truth is that, if a memorial campaign had been launched at almost any time in previous decades, it would have been shouted down. The Cold War, the Campaign for Nuclear Disarmament, the Vietnam War, the Peace Movement of the 1960s and 1970s: all made for an impossible climate for such an endeavour.

Ironically, it took another war, this time in Afghanistan, for the nation to rediscover its appreciation for our armed forces and the sacrifice made by so many young men and women and for the pendulum of public opinion to swing back to where it had been in 1945.

At long last, as the late Robin Gibb said in the song he wanted to perform at the unveiling, the families of 55,573 men won't 'cry alone'.

James Dunlop

Royal Air Force

Pilot

In the early hours of 11 October 1941 a No. 12 Squadron Vickers Wellington crash-landed on a Norfolk beach. There was a total loss of life when the bomber set off a mine. On board was second pilot Jamie Dunlop, who had, some months before, prepared a letter for his parents.

Sgt. Pilot Dunlop, J.L.S.
R67572
12/6/41

Dear Mother & Father
I have no reason to believe that this letter will ever be read since it will only be opened if and when I am killed, or at least listed among those who 'failed to return'. I have no feeling of impending fate so please do not feel that I knew what lay ahead of me when I wrote this. I know that my duty, not only to my country and humanity but to myself, lies ahead. I know that in carrying out my duty I must run great risks. Risks I may add that leave me little chance of seeing you again. Yet it is because of the risk, rather than any certainty, that I write this letter.

Firstly, I want you to realize and try even to be proud, that you have given a man to the cause of human liberty. Please

don't make the error of mourning me on account of my youth. That youthfulness is only apparent to you because you are considerably older than most parents with a son my age. Young as I am I have seen a great deal of this world and of the life of this world. I have lived in free countries among free peoples and have grown to manhood loving the liberty I have enjoyed. It has not been easy for me in life nor was freedom so widespread as it might have been for others. Still, progress was being made along the correct lines.

That progress must never be stopped by anyone or anything. All men must learn to live at peace with his fellow men and to grant all, regardless of station or birth, creed or color, the same rights and privileges which he himself deserves or enjoys.

Class distinction MUST be wiped out. Surely if there is a God, he did not intend that his creatures should live amid hate and distrust here on earth as a preparation to entering his kingdom. If we are to live with God we must learn first to live like God or as he would have us live. In other words we must work out our own Salvation. Jesus was and is the formula, it is up to us to follow the formula to [sic], and the same answer. By this I do not intend to condone the organized bodies of men & women which dictate the rules, judge the participants and ostracize the sinners. Each man to his own life, his own belief or lack thereof and to his own morals or code of ethics.

Since my early childhood I have tried to steer my own life along the path that led to the achievement of my ambition — to be a brain surgeon. There is no hope of that now but, as I explained to you once, my death may make it possible for some other lad to do the work I envisioned for myself. I go in that belief, be it vain or otherwise. Dropping bombs seems like a far cry from medicine yet I found it was my duty for once to 'be cruel to be kind'. I hate killing and suffering with all my soul yet I have killed and caused suffering. If I am to be excused it must be on the grounds that I killed the few to save the many. Nazism has, and would continue to destroy truth and independent thought, without which we must inevitably suffer and die. Die deaths of the soul and mind as well as the body! If there is no thought there is no freedom, no progress, no life.

If there is any message which the coming generation should have from mine let it be a message from us who have fought and died to make future generations of human beings possible. Let the message be this — we have cleared the site and laid the foundations — you build. This time let us hope they take the plans out of that hip pocket.

Well folks, I had better draw this to a close. This won't have been pleasant reading yet I want no tears on my behalf. I have done my duty — completed my life's work. If there be any honours or rewards due to me let them be these two, One: That you regard me as worthy of being your son. And Two: That there come to pass at last 'A Good Earth'.
Goodbye and God Bless you.

Your loving son,
Jamie.

Sources and Acknowledgements

Authors

Section 1 The Bomber Command Memorial *Robin Gibb, Jim Dooley, Gordon Rayner*
Section 2 Bomber Command At War *Steve Darlow*
Section 3 Bomber Operation *Sean Feast*
Section 4 Veterans in Portrait *Steve Darlow*
Section 5 They Gave Everything *Steve Darlow*

Published sources

Babbington Smith, C., *Evidence in Camera* (Chatto and Windus, 1957).
Bennett, D., *Pathfinder* (Frederick Muller Ltd, 1958).
Bond, S., Darlow, S., Evan-Hart, J., Feast, S., Purcell, A., and Yeoman, C., *Bomber Command: Failed to Return* (Fighting High, 2011).
Bowman, M., *RAF Bomber Stories* (Patrick Stephen Ltd, 1998).
Cheshire, L., *Bomber Pilot* (Hutchinson & Co. (Publishers) Ltd, 1943).
Darlow, S., *D-Day Bombers: The Veteran's Story* (Grub Street, 2004).
Darlow, S., *Lancaster Down!* (Grub Street, 2000).
Darlow, S., *Sledgehammers for Tintacks – Bomber Command Combats the V-1 Menace, 1943–1944* (Grub Street, 2002).
Darlow, S., *Special Op: Bomber* (David and Charles, 2008).
Farrell, A., *From Take-off to Touchdown* (Cirrus Associates, 1999).
Gibson, G., *Enemy Coast Ahead* (Goodall Publications Ltd, 1995).
Pearce, W. G. (Bill), *The Wing is Clipped* (Privately published, 1996).
Rivaz, R. C., *Tail Gunner* (Sutton Publishing, 2003).
Taylor, J., and Davidson, M., *Bomber Crew* (Hodder & Stoughton, 2004).

RAF Bomber Command: www.rafbombercommand.com
Bomber Command Museum of Canada: www.Bombercommandmuseum.ca
Spiritofcanada.com: www.bombercommandmuseum.ca/s,peenemunde.html

**'Voices from the conscience
Call us in our comfort zone
Cast that cloak of your contentment
Rise up and right that wrong.'**

The Bomber Command Memorial Board wishes to acknowledge the generous assistance of the following individuals and organizations in respect of the Bomber Command Memorial:

MRAF Sir Michael Beetham GCB CBE DFC AFC (President) • Malcolm White OBE (Chairman) • Sqn Ldr Tony Iveson DFC (Former Chairman) • Air Cdre Charles Clarke OBE (Former Chairman)
Doug Radcliffe MBE (Secretary) • Paul Mellor (Treasurer) • Alfred Huberman • Harry Irons DFC • Gordon Mellor • Peter Smith • Thomas Merriman • Bob McAllister • David Keen • Vivienne Hammer

James Dooley • Sir William Blackburne • Maj John Boyes TD • Sebastian Cox • Sophy Gardner MBE

John Caudwell • Lord Ashcroft KCMG • Richard Desmond • Robin Gibb CBE and The Heritage Foundation

Ministers of the Crown • The Governments of Australia, Canada and New Zealand • Commonwealth air force and veterans associations • The Polish Air Force Association
Le Ministère de la Défense et des Anciens Combattants, France

Liam O'Connor Architects • Philip Jackson CVO • C. J. Dudley DFC • Gilbert-Ash Ltd • S. McConnell and Sons • RadcliffesLeBrasseur • Richard Kindersley • Dave Martin Roofing Ltd

The RAF Benevolent Fund • The Royal Air Force • The Royal Air Force Museum • The Air Historical Branch • The RAF Club • City of London • Westminster City Council • Transport for London
The Royal Parks • The Daily Telegraph Group • The Express Group • George Gilmour (Metals) Ltd • Norsk Hydro • The London Taxi Drivers Association • The Venerable Brian Lucas CB • Caroline Coles
Caroline Davies • Dave Yule • Mark Wasilewski • Ollie Smith • Wg Cdr Philip Lamb • The Venerable Ray Pentland QHC • Tano Rea • Chris Pickthall • David Forsyth • Brian Finch • David Graham.

Jane Alexander • Rupert Armitage • Jane Bailey • Pat Barnard • Bob Bennett MBE • Dean Benton • Simon Betts • Jane Binley • Nigel Blair-Park • Ernie Bohm • Alan Bradley • Duncan and Carla Butler
Jane Casebury • Lord Craig of Radley GCB OBE DSc MA • Wendy Craig • Andrew Critchley • Sir Stephen Dalton KCB AD RAF • John Davies • Peter Davies • Brenda Dooley • Frank Dooley
Gerry Dooley • Joe Dooley • John Dooley • Tim Drake • Iain Duncan Smith MP • Alton Edwards • Sam Espensen • Alan Frame • Ann-Mari Freebairn • Tony Gallagher • Marco Giannangeli • Dwina Gibb
RJ Gibb • Dennis Gimes • Howard Goldstein • Curtis Goring • Robert Hardman • Neil Hodges • Gerald Howarth MP • Georgie Howlett • Paul Hughesdon • Louise Hyam • John Ingham • Mark Jaimes
Gareth Jones • Kevan Jones MP • Sean Kelly • Karl Kjarsgaard • Will Lewis • Justin Llewellyn (and Champagne Taittinger) • Charles Lucas • Andrew MacIntosh • Murdoch Maclennan • Barry McCann
Jane McDonald • Vicki Michelle • Lord Morris of Manchester • Alistair Moss • Dave Most • Mike Neville • Chris Newell • Phil O'Dell • Amber Organ • Simon Osbourne, Flt Lt Anthony Parkinson •
Katharine Patel • John Penrose MP • Nicky Philipps • Sqn Ldr Al Pinner • Tom Portet • Merril Powell • Bianca Rainbow • Gordon Rayner • Mike Read • Craig Riley • Sue Riley • Andrew Robathan MP
Air Cdre Mark Roberts • John Romain • Finbarr Ronayne • Charlie Ross • Danny Saxon • Mike Scott • David Shepherd • Mandy Shepherd • Sqn Ldr Ian Smith • Howard Snell • Sarah Stewart
Richard Stuckes • Rod Temperton • Stephanie Thomas • Sir Glenn Torpy GCB CBE DSO ADC • Viscount Trenchard of Wolfeton DL • Carol Vorderman MBE • Madonna Walsh • Augusta Westland
Nigel White • Tori White • Hugh Whittow • David Willetts • Vivienne Woods • Air Mshl Sir Robert Wright KBE, AFC.

Blake • Blink Airways • The Goring Hotel • The Lanesborough Hotel • The Lime Centre • Littlehampton Welding • Mango Bay Hotel, Barbados • Marshalls of Cambridge • Mobility Bureau
Richard Austin Alloys • Warner Bros Music.

In addition to the acknowledgements above, the publishers would also like to thank the following people for their assistance with this book:

An extended thank you to Caroline Davies who has been instrumental in ensuring this book became a reality. We also wish to acknowledge the invaluable support of Jim Dooley, for his continued support, and Sebastian Cox, for his guidance. Andrew Hayden and Russell Thompson also deserve special mention for backing this book project and making it a reality.

Our sincerest appreciation goes to our featured 'Veterans in Portrait':

John Banfield • John Bell • George Dunn • Dave Fellowes • Igraine Hamilton • Harry Irons • Gordon Mellor • Eileen Richards • Arthur Smith • Buzz Spilman • Jack Watts
Geoffrey Whitehead • Calton Younger

For their general assistance we thank:

John Beeching • Dean Black • Adam Darlow • Michael Darlow • Maggie Darlow • David Dunlop • Sally Dunlop • Scott Dunlop • Lisa Dwyer • Christina Gale • Michael Garbutt • Cherry Greveson
Eric and Jean Hammal • John and Gayle Heselwood • Sally Hughes • Steve Kitchener and Graham Calvert (of Parallel Lines) • Linda Meredith • Tracy Neal • Declan O'Flanagan • Anna Parkinson
Margot Rowling • Lois Watts-Sculthorpe • Rachael Smith • Shern Spilman • Stevenston Historical Society • Penny Whitehead

For supplying photographs we thank:

Lee Barton (Air Historical Branch) • Jonathan Buckmaster • Nick Carter ('Victory' inscription image, page 4) • Tim Clarke • Sam Espensen • Paul Grover • Tim Humphries (Astonleigh Studio)
Gareth Jones • Peter Mares • Doug McKenzie • Neil Perrin • Simply Photography • Ronnie Raeside (www.raesidephoto.co.uk) • Jim Selby (Express Newspapers) • Mark Tomlin (Flipside Group)

For providing photographs of relatives killed in action we extend our appreciation to:

Chris Beare • Linzee Druce • Susan Dugas • Nicola Gaughan • John Green • Robin Hood • Dom Howard • Jo Lewis • Fairfax Luxmoore • Gerald Marsh • Liz Moyle • Nicki Richards
Ian Robertson • Barbara Shotliff